Brian Greenaway was president of a Hell's Angel chapter. He was violent, full of hate, deeply into drugs.

Then, in Dartmoor Prison, he had an experience which changed him completely.

This is Brian's own story – powerful, sometimes ugly but real. It describes his tough early years, his dramatic conversion and his struggles to work out a new way of life.

Brian Greenaway is now a full-time missionary to men in prison. He can be contacted by letter to PO Box 448, London, SW19 6SD.

Brian Kellock is a journalist and deacon of a west-country Baptist church.

HELL'S Angel

BRIAN GREENAWAY
with Brian Kellock

A LION PAPERBACK

Tring • Batavia • Sydney

Copyright © 1982 Brian Greenaway and Brian Kellock

Published by
Lion Publishing plc
Icknield Way, Tring, Herts, England
ISBN 0 85648 389 3
Albatross Books Pty Ltd
PO Box 320, Sutherland, NSW 2232, Australia
ISBN 0 86760 360 7

First edition 1982
Reprinted twice 1982
Reprinted 1983, 1984, 1985, 1986, 1988

Printed and bound in Great Britain by
Collins, Glasgow

CONTENTS

1
THE FIGHT

I started running up the beach, stumbling over the pebbles in the dark as I went. Someone on the promenade was shouting.

'Hey Brian, come on! We've got some skinheads.'

I reached the wall and pulled myself up over the edge. The stiletto knife hidden in my sleeveless denim jacket thumped against the white railings. Excitement mixed with anger was already making the adrenalin flow. As president of the Leigh Park Hell's Angels I should have been up front leading the way but I'd been caught off guard.

Thirty of us had motorbiked in convoy from Portsmouth to Bognor that evening expecting to find a beach barbeque and some action. We'd got there about ten but there was no barbeque and no action. Everyone was uptight as we parked our bikes and it was my fault. Frustrated, I had left the others on the promenade and gone down to the water's edge. Now, by the time I rejoined the rest of my mates, the fighting had begun.

Afterwards Fat Mick, my lieutenant and closest friend, told me how it had started. As he and Crazy Jim and the others went on ahead of me towards the town, lipping anyone who got in their way, three skinheads came out through the side door of a pub. Seeing our gang, one of them dived back inside. Within seconds skinheads were pouring out onto the pavement and into the main drag. Quickly the numbers were even. Hell's Angels and skinheads pitched in together, scattering the passers-by. It was fight on sight.

Fists, bike chains and stones were all flying by the time I got there. And more skinheads kept spewing out of the pub. It was like a funnel in reverse. They were all tooled-up for fighting. Some were armed with cricket stumps. One of them, taller and even more ugly than the rest, with ears like open taxi doors, had a bat. He used it later to break my nose. Soon we were outnumbered. Afterwards I found out that this place was their headquarters. There were 200 inside on the night we showed up.

The blood began to flow. We couldn't hold them off and one by one we began to drop back. Crazy Jim staggered by me. A rock had gashed his cheek. Blood from the short but deep cut covered the side of his face. The sight of it freaked me out. I smashed my fist into the face of the guy who had been chasing him. He went down hard. Together Jim and I moved back again. Behind me six skinheads were laying into someone's bird.

By now all fear had gone. I was pretty mindless and could feel no pain. Into the fighting pile I leapt, drop-kicking the biggest of the attackers, putting both boots into his face. The bird scrambled to her feet and ran. So did I.

None of us liked backing out of a fight. We had won too many in the past. But here we had no choice. We must have been outnumbered five or six to one and even for Leigh Park Hell's Angels the odds were too great. Anyone staying around was going to get killed. Only by getting back to our bikes would we be safe. The other guys all had solos and had parked them several hundred yards back along the front, against the kerb. But mine was a combo, a Panther 600 I'd bought only the week before. So I had parked it in a car park away from the rest. That was my big mistake.

In the poorly-lit car park were just two cars and my combo. On three sides was a high brick wall, hardly visible in the darkness. Along the front ran a white painted fence. I raced in through the car park's only entrance and slid to a halt on the gravel by my bike. As I jumped on to the foot rest and kicked the engine over the bike leaped forward and stalled. I had forgotten I'd left it in gear. The gear lever jammed and frantically I tried to free it. So frantically that I did not notice I had been followed.

Wham! The cricket bat crashed across my face, breaking my nose and releasing a torrent of blood that poured down on to my shirt and open jacket. As I regained my balance and my eyes cleared I saw that I was surrounded by skinheads. How many I don't know but my escape route through to the car park exit was blocked.

The guy with the cricket bat was getting ready to have another swing. With the pain in my face I went berserk. There was no escape. I would kill or be killed. Quicker than anyone could see, my right hand released the popper securing the seven-inch-long double-edged stiletto in my jacket. Its sheath was sewn in at an angle on the left side. The handle of the knife pointed downwards at an angle towards the buckle on my belt.

In one movement the knife was in my hand, moving out of its sheath and swinging downwards. Cleanly and silently it sliced through the stomach of the guy with the bat. Just as silently he fell, without a cry or a moan. He must have passed straight out with the pain.

'That's got you!' I screamed.

One of his mates moved forward, not knowing he'd been knifed. He spat on his hands ready for the fight. Down again went my knife. This time it went straight into his stomach and down went the second guy as silently as the first. Now my only thought was to destroy everyone around me.

'Come on, I'll kill the lot of you!'

Standing upright on my footrests I let go with all the obscenities I knew. But by now the rest of the skinheads had seen the knife and, realizing what had already happened, they began to fall back. I jumped from my bike, swinging the knife around me. A pathway to the exit opened up as the bodies moved back. I ran through them out on to the promenade, past an ambulance which must have been called as soon as the fighting had started, and past a police car whose three occupants looked more like specta- tors than peacekeepers. I ran on up the front to where my mates were waiting.

'Quick!' I shouted. 'Hide this.'

Tiny, who was anything but small, took the knife I handed to him and rammed it hard up between the saddle and fuel tank of his Super 6 Suzuki.

'I'll dump that later,' was all he said.

Then, not really thinking what I was asking him to do, I called to Fat Mick, 'Go and get my bike out of there.'

I knew he wouldn't dare refuse. Before he went he passed me his jacket. Any other time he would be proud to show off the colours so neatly sewn into it. They were the badge of a real Hell's Angel. But this time it was different. Soon he was back, with the bike and a fat grin on his face. The skinheads had been too busy fussing around their dying friends to worry about him.

It was as though we had been forgotten.

The bang which broke my nose dulled all senses except the sense of pain. Shakily I lit a cigarette, put the bike into gear and rode to the front of the line of waiting bikes. With me leading the way, the gang moved off along the prom- enade towards home. No one tried to stop us.

Calmed by the inhaled marijuana I began to feel safe. No need to hurry. There was no feeling of concern for the suffering we were leaving behind and no fear in my mind of being caught. If I had been a bit more anxious I would not have chosen the most direct route out of the town.

For two miles we were alone, passing first shops and then houses and a park. A police car came by at speed going the way we had just come. Its roof lights were flashing and siren wailing. My head cleared as I sensed that we were heading for trouble. Around a slow right-hand bend the road ahead was blocked with cars. We were riding right into the action.

Suddenly I laughed. It was like a comic opera. Between us and the road-block a side street led off into a housing estate. One by one we peeled off the main road . . . me, Fat Mick, Crazy Jim, Tiny, with the others following close behind. I thought we had been clever but there was no way out of the maze of roads we had just entered. We were riding into a trap.

Each biker was on his own. I finished up ringed around by half a dozen lock-up garages. Several police cars had followed us on to the estate so there was nowhere to go but into hiding. Two other Hell's Angels, one with a bird riding pillion, followed me in. We dumped the bikes and ran to the darkness at the back of the garages.

Around us house lights were coming on. The bike noises died down but cars were still moving in the streets and there were occasional shouts as someone's hiding-place was found by the police. We kept close in the shadows of the garages and waited.

Behind us, barely visible, rough open ground smelt of thrown-away rubbish. Farther back I could make out the thin lines of a high wire fence and a line of trees. Our only way out was the way we came in. For the second time in one night I was trapped. Only this time it was my real enemy, the law, which had me cornered. Skinheads were just guys to be stamped on for kicks, but I had a hatred for the pigs that at twenty-three was already turning me paranoid. It was their kind of authority I had been fighting against since I was eight. First with my mother and stepfather, then at the children's home, the detention centre and finally in prison.

A car went by the entrance to the garages, its headlights briefly lighting up the side-wall of a house. It came back and stopped. A door opened and slammed shut and a copper appeared at the entrance, silhouetted against the street lights. With his torch he quickly examined each garage-front in turn.

'No one here.' His voice was rather too loud to be convincing. A door slammed again and the car drove off. It was a common dodge.

'Keep quiet,' I whispered.

Too late. The bird giggled nervously.

Suddenly the copper reappeared. Behind him were several others. This time he came cautiously towards the garages. He knew where to look and soon picked out the first of us in the light of his torch as we tried to press against the garage wall.

'Come out you . . . and you . . . and you.'

There was excitement in his voice. He obviously hadn't expected to find four of us in one place. There was more excitement as we came out into the light. Now my blood-covered jacket and shirt could be clearly seen. Although I was off my territory and the police here didn't know me or my reputation for violence, the sight of that blood convinced them on the spot that I had done the knifing.

'This is the one.' A big copper grabbed my arm.

'Now you're for it.'

I bluffed it out with a laugh.

Quickly but cautiously they pinned me against their car and frisked me, looking for a knife and finding a rolled-up bike chain. I was on my own and outnumbered four to one. When they told me to get into the car I did as I was told rather than risk getting my head kicked. It had happened before.

The ride back to Bognor police station was short but uncomfortable, handcuffed between two pigs even bigger than me. As we approached the station I nearly lost my bottle for the first time since the fight. Skinheads lined the steps and blocked the entrance. More inside the building littered the reception.

'They've got Greenaway!'

Someone had recognized me. I knew how it would have gone if my gang had been there and it was a skinhead they were bringing in for stabbing my mates. Law or no law we would have gone for him. I felt the tension rising. There were angry jeers and jostling and a couple of attempts to put the boot in. My escorts were getting nervous as they dragged me, pushed me, through to the safety of a questioning cell. I wasn't sorry to get there either.

There the questioning began – a battle of wits at which I had become an expert. I also learned what had happened to the two guys I'd stabbed. Both were alive but critically ill. After emergency operations to stitch them up, each had to have a second operation.

'You'll be lucky if they live,' I was told.

I didn't give a damn! They would be the lucky ones, not me, I thought.

The questioning about the fighting and the blood went on all night. I got no sleep. No one believed that all the blood on me was mine and even I wasn't sure. Only later did forensic tests show that it was. And long before that they had got more than enough eyewitness evidence to charge me with unlawful and malicious wounding and possessing an offensive weapon. They also had me for possessing stolen goods. This last charge made me chuckle. I had borrowed my mate's tax disc for my new bike.

For the next six weeks I was detained. The police would not agree to bail and I didn't blame them. I had jumped it before and this time the charge was serious. There were frequent visits to court before I was finally sentenced to eighteen months in prison. It could have been life for all I cared. I was so emotionally cold and uncaring by then. Violence had become a part of my everyday life. It was the only way I knew of hitting back at those who had leaned so heavily on me since those early, loveless and bitter childhood days spent in the Hampshire village of Steep.

2
HOME FROM HOME!

My father left home when I was four, driven away by my mother's arguing and moodiness. She had a temper that would flare up at the least excuse. Not that *his* temper was all that even, and she usually finished up getting a thrashing.

When he left, my younger sister Sheila was two and there was another baby on the way. Each Saturday he would come back, not to our house but to his sister's, two doors away. We lived away from the centre of the village, like a colony of working-class lepers. A triangle of grey concrete-slab council houses surrounded our 'playground' of well-worn grass and three oak trees.

Often I sat on the kerb outside our house chasing the dust with a stick and hoping my father would stop and say 'Hello son' as he drove by. But he never did. Because of the bitterness between him and my mother he blanked me out completely. It hurt so much I can still feel it.

He did come back to the house once. It was in the evening. We were all upstairs and the doors were bolted. A noise like someone scraping came from the kitchen. Mum was so scared she sent me down to see what it was. My father was trying to get into the house by taking the putty from a kitchen window.

'For God's sake,' screamed my mother when I told her, 'let him in before he breaks the glass!'

We didn't have enough money for food, let alone for a

new window pane. As I unbolted the door he pushed it open fiercely and showed his thanks by grabbing my arm. Pulling it hard up behind my back, he had me screaming all the way up the stairs. My mother had shut herself in the bedroom but came out when she heard my cries.

They rowed. He belted her around the room and then left, with my mother screaming after him down the stairs and my sister crying. I just stood on the landing shaking with fear and anger. Afterwards we sometimes saw him in the village and once he gave Sheila and me a ride in his car but he never came to the house again.

Although I didn't learn much at school there was one thing I learnt very early. If you hadn't got a dad at home then you got blamed for everything that went wrong. It didn't make sense but it was true. If a window got broken or another boy's pencil went missing, I was blamed.

And it wasn't much better at home. Once when a neighbour told my mother I'd broken a window she gave me a belting that left me sore for days. But she didn't think to ask me if I had done it.

Quickly I became the villain of the village. If I was going to get hit around the head with a saucepan it might as well be for something I had done. And it didn't stop at breaking windows. Breaking into shops and unoccupied houses became more my line. The way I acted didn't make me very popular with the grown-ups and the other kids were offhand most of the time. I often knew what it was to be lonely.

For me, the one good thing about living in the country was being able to escape to the surrounding woods. I grew to love the open fields and quiet woods which rose behind the house. But not only for their beauty. There I could get away from the pointing fingers of grown-ups and the persecution of the other kids. When the weather was good I would climb the hill after school and wander among the trees or through the long grass at the edge of the meadow until forced home by darkness or hunger.

One evening when I was eight, I came home from the woods to find a stranger sitting in the living-room in our only easy chair. Sheila and my youngest sister sat shyly at the dining-table which filled the middle of the room. My mother came in from the kitchen when I shut the front door and stood behind me. I stared across the living-room at the man in the collarless shirt, sitting uneasily on the edge of the chair. She spoke without expression.

'This is your new dad.' Her voice sounded like I had a new dad every day. I stared, angry and resentful. Turning to face my mother all I could think to say was 'Isn't he ugly'. And I meant it. It wasn't just his long, wiry body and the sharp features of his face that turned me off him. At that age I resented the idea of another male in the house. Up till now I had been the man, doing the man's jobs and staying up in the evening to keep my mother company until she went to bed.

She wasn't much of a talker but we would sit together in the evening listening to the radio after the other two had been sent to bed. I kept out of the way while they were got ready and hoped that I wouldn't be remembered until she was sitting down. On cold winter evenings she would pull her chair up to the Rayburn solid fuel fire and, with its doors wide open, sit a few feet away from it soaking up the heat. The rest of the room remained cold and only when she left the room would I dare close the doors of the fire to let it burn up.

My mother worked at times in school kitchens, but mostly we lived off social security. We were too hard up to afford coal for the fire – unless it fell into the road outside from a lorry delivering nearby. If it did I had to be quick to get out there first. I would feel pleased with myself if I could get back indoors with half a bucket of coal to give my mother.

Mostly we burned whatever we could get from the woods behind the house. In the autumn and winter months all the kids, and some of the grown-ups, pushed ancient prams up the steep path leading to the wood, sometimes spending a whole Saturday morning loading them up with twigs, bark, rotting wood and anything else that would burn and not be missed. It was one of the few times I was able to mix in with the other kids and I took great pride in being in charge of our four-wheeled transporter.

With a stepfather around I lost a lot of these jobs which made me feel useful at home. It was the same with the front garden which I had enjoyed trying to keep tidy. But worse still, I now had two grown-ups to knock me about instead of just one. More than once my new father was told that he was only there to keep me under control. He certainly worked hard enough at it. It was no fun being chased around the wilderness of a back garden from two directions at once and having to decide quickly which pair of flying arms would land on me the lightest.

I soon got to hate him and I often tried to take it out on her. It was her fault he had come. Not that it got me very far. In my frustration I would race out through the kitchen where she was working, out into the back garden shouting something like, 'You stupid cow'. Once I didn't make it to the kitchen door quickly enough, and was left facing her coming at me with a broom high in the air. Down came the handle. Wham! The arm I put up to protect myself got broken.

I was twelve when the first probation officer arrived on the scene. I got caught breaking in through the window of a big house on the other side of the village and was put on probation for three years. Although I didn't like getting caught or having to go to the Magistrates' Court in Petersfield two-and-a-half miles away, I did enjoy the probation officer coming to visit me at home. For the first time ever I found someone who seemed to care about what happened to me. During his visits we would talk about my future. If

I got the chance I told him how I was being treated. I also spoke about my plans to join the navy.

We got on well and I trusted him. I believe he even trusted me. He took seriously my cries for help. I told him I thought I would finish up hanging from a rope. It was the sort of melodramatic thing a lonely kid would say but he obviously sensed the desperation behind it. It was his idea that I should go to a children's home. He said I would be better off there and it would be good training for a life at sea, living amongst a larger group of boys. I think he just wanted to get me away from the beatings at home.

Without any trouble, the probation officer talked my mother into letting me move to a children's home in Southampton. For me, the attraction was that it was near the docks and the ships which I dreamt of as my escape route. For them the attraction was just getting me out of their way. Unlike my sisters, I had always been a bother to them and now that I had been stupid enough to get caught by the law, they couldn't get rid of me fast enough. It never occurred to them that they might be partly to blame.

On a bright, cold day in October my probation officer drove me the forty miles into the centre of Southampton. I had never been so far before and I treated it as a big adventure. Although the home was not far from the docks it was in a pleasant and quiet part of the city away from busy traffic even though there was a British Road Services' lorry-yard next door. It was certainly a big contrast to the green and open countryside around the village I had left behind. But during the early days I was just glad to be away from the cruelty of my parents and I didn't miss the green hills.

The home was for boys. It was run by a freaky supervisor and his easy-going wife. Looking back, I picture him like some character out of Dickens, long, thin, grey and stooped and often with a billiard cue in his hand. They had two daughters, one my age and one a bit younger. I soon got keen on the older one and by the time I left two years later we had quite a love session going.

The white-painted house stood alone, with lawns at the front and high ivy-covered walls either side. A gravel drive led from the road to the front entrance and to the back of the house. On the ground floor of the house was the supervisor's office and living accommodation. Behind them were the dining-room and games-room and further back still, a laundry-room and a boiler house, which became my own private retreat.

There were fifteen boys in the home most of the time I was there. The two eldest were twins without parents. They were the good guys. It didn't take me long to find out that just about everyone else was into something bad, mostly thieving. Each Saturday morning they would go into the city centre in twos to spend their weekly pocket-money. That didn't take long and the rest of the things they came home with were lifted without being paid for. Sometimes it was heavy stuff that could have caused a lot of aggravation with the law. There were even hands going into the tills and ripping out notes.

Soon the 'super' got wise to what was going on. It was probably when he caught them all swopping their prizes after a morning's 'shopping'. After that he lay in wait for them and anybody caught with stolen goods got walloped with his billiard cue. Strange though it seems now, I didn't get involved in any of this – partly because I'd been frightened of the Petersfield magistrate but mostly because I preferred being alone down by the docks, watching the ships.

That didn't mean I escaped the billiard cue. At least once I remember he went for me with it for cheeking him. I remember it because he came off worse. As I put up my arm to protect myself, I hit him in the mouth. It wasn't on purpose but he thought it was and it made him mad. He steamed off to his office and left me standing in the hall for more than half an hour. When he came out he completely blanked me. I don't think I'd really scared him but some of the other lads were beginning to feel their weight. In particular there was one black guy who freaked out without any warning. Maybe the 'super' thought I was following their example. He never leaned heavily on me again.

There wasn't much caring or sign of love in the home and I began to realize that I was no better off here than back at Steep. But it wasn't all punishment and discipline – mostly thanks to the twins. They took me along to Boys' Brigade at a nearby Baptist Church where they were both officers. Because I came from a home no one insisted that I went to church on Sundays, so I just enjoyed the weeknight activities and the parades.

The twins were also good musicians. They played the oboe, flute, fife and drums and they tried to teach me to play the fife. I got a great kick out of this and spent hours practising alone away from everybody else, down in the drying-room next to the boiler. Back home I had escaped to the woods. Here the drying-room was my refuge from other people.

But even the twins could not help my loneliness. My mother came only three times to see me at the home. Remembering how easily she and my stepfather had parted with me I had no reason to feel wanted in the world.

From my room I could see over the high wall that separated the house from the lorry-park next door. Early in the morning I would watch drivers sheeting up their loads, revving up their diesel engines and driving out through the yard gates and away to places I could not begin to imagine. Seeing them go made me feel desperately lonely. Looking out on to the yard I would cry, wishing to God that I could crawl underneath one of the tarpaulins and be driven off. It didn't matter where, so long as it was away from the home.

3
SHOCK SENTENCE

Escape from the children's home came soon enough. At fifteen I was allowed to go. After a train ride to London to collect a new suit and a cardboard case, I was on my own – except for my old probation officer. We had kept in touch. By now I had lost interest in going to sea so he got me a job back home in Steep.

This meant living with my mother and stepfather again. I wasn't happy about it but I didn't have any choice. There was no way I was going to get a job on my own. In two years I had grown quite a bit and he probably reckoned I now knew how to take care of myself. But the truth was that the strict discipline at the home together with a lot of bullying at school left me less able to stand up for myself than when I left the village. Instead of defending myself by arguing I just kept quiet. Only when I was made very angry would I lash out – usually with my fist.

The job he got me was on a construction site. A new reservoir was being built above the village. It was hard work but I liked being in the open air. From high above the village I could look across the open country to Petersfield.

If the job was good, living at home wasn't. Six months of fighting and quarrelling was as much as I could stand. The crunch came one Tuesday evening after work. It was the beginning of winter and bitterly cold. As I came up the path at the back of the house I could hear the familiar quarrelling voices in the kitchen. Hesitantly I turned the handle on the kitchen door and opened it. My father had a milk bottle raised above my mother's head.

He turned quickly as I came in. Milk from the bottle ran down his arm. The brightness of his eyes betrayed that he was freaking out. This was a row to finish all the rows and they were both going overboard fast. I had to act quickly or the bottle was going to land on my mother's head.

As I rushed in, my father swung his free fist at me and hit the bridge of my nose with his knuckles. The blood began to run – and so did I! I had stopped my mother from having her head opened but now I was scared what he would do to me. Through the front door I went, screaming over my shoulder to my mother,

'I'm going to call the police!'

He began to panic.

'Don't do it. Stop!'

He sounded afraid and I hadn't expected that. Inside I felt a sudden surge of power. If I had stopped running then and not gone to the phone things might have improved between us. But while I kept going, the advantage was mine. He was still some way behind me as I pulled open the phone-box door and lifted the receiver. He stopped, turned and walked towards the village.

When I got back my mother was working at the sink. It was as though nothing had happened. Shortly afterwards a police car pulled up outside.

'Tell them to go away!' my mother snapped.

'But what about him?' I asked in answer to her command. I was afraid he would go for her or me again when he got back and I didn't want another bloody nose.

'You called them; you get rid of them,' was all she said. She made no secret of her dislike for the police. I had to tell them to go away, but with tears and blood on my face it wasn't easy. The two young policemen could do nothing. It was a family row and since it had ended with no one seriously hurt they were powerless. But they asked enough questions to know what had been going on.

'If there is any more bother, you let us know.'

They backed up and drove away towards Petersfield, leaving behind a feeling that was strange to me. All other contacts with the law had left me sore or angry. But this time I sensed they had a real concern for my safety.

Before I got back inside the house I had decided I'd had enough. I was going to leave. After all, I was being treated like a lodger and I could just as easily be a lodger somewhere else, or so I thought as I made plans to go.

While I was at the children's home I spent my holidays with my gran on the Isle of Wight. There I met a bird who lived in Northampton. We had kept in touch and now that I had decided to quit Steep I phoned saying I wanted to see her. She'd left school in the summer and was working as a cleaner in a hospital near her home town. I said I would meet her there on Saturday.

The day after the fight I gave in my notice and told my mother I was leaving home. She said nothing that would have changed my mind. Mentally the message was 'If you want to go, go.' On Friday I got my pay and early on Saturday morning caught the bus to Petersfield railway station to begin the 140-mile journey to Northampton. The bus and rail tickets took most of my money. The rest I wanted for food, so I walked the two miles from Northampton station to the hospital. There I had a long wait outside the main gate until she finished work.

Although she was only a kid, she knew her way around and soon found me somewhere to stay. It was a small and poorly furnished bed-sit where the only way to cook anything was on a plug-in electric hotplate. No pots, no pans, no nothing. On Monday I bluffed my way into a job working on a machine grinding car valves in a factory not far away from my digs.

At sixteen I was looking after myself for the first time

and soon found I wasn't very good at it. Half my wages went on rent. I couldn't cook and had nothing but the hotplate to heat things on, so it was mostly soup and bread and coffee. If I went into the town I'd nick a couple of tins of canned food with meat in them.

Living on poor food and too little of it, I soon became weak and ill. I had diarrhoea nearly all the time and couldn't keep warm. Christmas came and it began to snow like I'd never seen it snow before – it was the winter of 1962. To get to work I had to walk through a park. Forcing myself through the snow I felt so ill that everything seemed unreal. I needed proper food and warmth but had very little money.

Then I remembered the dress studs. One had a diamond in the middle and the other a pearl. A couple of months before, while still at home, I had broken into an empty house with an old school mate of mine who lived in another village five miles away. We had lifted a travelling clock and a silver teapot which we managed to sell for a fiver each. Without telling him, I had pocketed two studs I found in the drawer of a dressing-table. These I brought with me to Northampton. They may not have been of any value but they looked good. I thought I might get something for them.

There was a jeweller I passed on the road into the town. Perhaps he could give me a price. Too stupid and desperate to have any fears, I walked boldly into the shop the next Saturday morning. With the diamond stud in my hand I asked the middle-aged man behind the counter how much he would give me for it.

'Where did you get this from?' There was suspicion in his eyes and in his voice. I mumbled something lame about getting it from my grandmother but I knew I had been rumbled. Like an idiot, I had already told him where I was living. Keeping hold of the pin, he said, 'Come back to-morrow. I'll have to do some tests on it.'

I didn't go back. The heat was on and I didn't want to

get caught again. Without even telling my bird, I packed my cardboard case and caught the train back to Portsmouth again. I was naive enough to think that I had got away with it.

If I learned anything at Northampton, it was that fending for yourself was hell. I was determined that the next job I got would be one where I was fed and looked after. I don't remember how, but I found just the job at a hotel in East Wittering near Chichester, working as a kitchen porter. Here life began to get better. I was fed properly, my health rapidly improved and I was no longer lonely!

Near the hotel was a café where motor-bike boys met. I didn't have a bike but the guys accepted me and I spent a lot of my time with them. The big attraction for me was the sound and the power of the machines they rode. What wouldn't I give to have a bike of my own between my legs, to feel the vibration and power of an engine! It was the beginning of an interest which became a passion and re- sulted five years later in the formation of the Leigh Park Hell's Angels.

If I made friends at Wittering, I also made enemies. I began to discover inside me the same violent temper I despised in my mother. Unable to argue with words, I didn't waste time trying to use them. Arguments could be settled more quickly with my fist. Even a friendly greeting I would misunderstand. One guy I knuckled in the local just for saying 'All right, pal'. To him it was a greeting. To me it was a threatening gesture. I thought this guy was coming on fresh with me, so I hit him hard in the mouth.

It soon got around that I was schizoid. And the more it spread the tougher I acted. Even the people I knew weren't safe. I had a mate at the hotel. He was a kitchen porter too. On our evenings off we went to the pub together. It was an ego trip for me to pretend I was drunk on half a glass of shandy. Coming home I would sometimes put on the full act.

Staggering home one evening after the pub closed, this mate started getting clever, laying into me with his fists. He thought I was too far gone to notice. It began to rain. Locked together we staggered into a shop doorway. His arm was round my neck and his punches got harder and harder. Suddenly it was no longer a joke. I freaked out and weighed into him full belt with both fists. As he went down I walked away leaving him slumped where he fell. For the short time I remained at East Wittering after that I was labelled as freaky.

And it was a short time. Events were catching up with me. About a year after quitting Northampton I was called into the hotel owner's office. I didn't know it then, but he was an ex-superintendent from Scotland Yard. With him in the office was a much younger man who turned out to be a detective. This newcomer swung round as I came in. He spoke sharply.

'You Brian Greenaway?'

I nodded.

'Have you ever lived in Northampton?'

He must have seen me react and had no need for an answer.

He then started asking about the diamond pin. Did I take it to such and such a jeweller? Where did I get it from? I began to try getting round the questions by lying. But he knew too much to believe any of it. Soon he had me in tears.

'Do you know how much that diamond pin was worth?'

I shook my head.

'£200!'

His interrogation was complete. The tough outer shell I had recently adopted rapidly crumbled and I was left crying bitterly with self pity. Putting my hand into my jacket pocket I pulled out the pearl pin which I still kept on me all the time.

'You'd better take this one as well,' I said, hoping it would make things easier. It probably made things worse.

Once again I was back at Petersfield Magistrates' Court. To my surprise my stepfather turned up and began sticking up for me at the hearing. Even the police went easy on me in their statements. I began to relax. It looked like I was going to have to put up with another spell on probation. I could not have been more wrong.

The shock sentence was three months in Gosport detention centre. It didn't mean much to me then but the expression on other people's faces told me it was bad news. My stepfather was nearly crying and the two coppers given the job of looking after me got very agitated. They knew I had been hit hard. I was just seventeen. For me the next three months were to be a cruel foretaste of prison life and a big influence on the sort of person I was to become.

4
PRISON

We drove into the detention centre and the high tubular gates closed behind us. Inside were well-kept lawns, white-painted kerbs and a tidy tarmac parade ground. In those first moments I sussed it out – there was something bad about the place. It didn't keep this tidy by itself.

The police car which had brought me the twenty miles from Petersfield Magistrates' Court pulled up outside a single storey reception building. My two escorts took me inside. They handed my papers and personal things to a middle-aged man in uniform sitting behind a high desk.

'Your name Brian Greenaway?'

I nodded.

'Check that all your things are here.'

One pen, one comb, one wallet, so much money. . . . He wrote every item down before putting them all in a bag. My two escorts wished me luck and left. With them went my freedom. For the first time in my life I was a prisoner.

'Take your clothes off.'

The officer pointed to a bin alongside his desk. As he watched each piece of clothing going into the bin he kept writing. Shirt, trousers, socks, shoes. . .

'Come on, everything off.'

He spoke quietly, with no more than a glance up from his desk. Only when I was naked did he look me up and down.

'Turn round.'

Embarrassed by his stare, I did as he told me. As I turned to face him again he handed me two blankets, a pillow and a pile of clothes which was my new uniform. I put the clothes on quickly.

'Ever done any marching?' he asked in a quiet voice.

I mumbled that I had been in the Air Training Corp at school. He moved to a window overlooking the parade ground and pointed to a building on the other side.

'See that door. You are going to march over there now. And march PROPLY.'

Suddenly he changed. Up till that point he had been a reasonable guy who seemed to have little interest in me. But now I was seeing my first screw on an ego trip.

'And if you don't do it *proply*,' he said again, stressing the last word, 'we'll stay here all day until you do.'

I got it right first time. From then on I marched everywhere.

Life at the centre was very physical with exercises, circuit training and weight-lifting every day, often at the double. At first I resented the harsh morning exercises. But as I grew more fit I began to enjoy it. By the time I left, my leg muscles had developed so much that the trousers I came in with only just fitted me.

Before breakfast we would be in the gym or out on the parade ground doing bunny hops. Hopping around on your haunches with hands behind your back gets very painful. The blood stops circulating in your legs after the first fifteen minutes. Whatever I did, whether it was bunny hops or press-ups, the instructor made sure I put all my effort into it; otherwise it would have to be done again. And each time I ran the mile it had to be faster than the time before. The lesson I learned was not to do my best the first time, so that there was room for improvement.

Once during my stay at Gosport my mother visited me. The only bit I remember was after we had said goodbye. I was brought out from my side of the visiting-room and

made to march past her on the way back to my quarters.
Left, right, left, right, arms straight and up to the shoulder.
I dared not look at her but as I passed I heard her giggle.
She had been embarrassed by what I was doing.

For the first week or so at the detention centre, evenings
are spent in a single cubicle. This is so that they can keep
an eye on you. It was easy to see why. The week I was in,
the guy in the next cubicle slashed both his wrists. I saw
him lying on his bed, both arms hanging over the edge. A
pool of blood was on the floor and more blood had con-
gealed over the wounds. He spent most of his detention in
the sick bay. From sleeping in a cubicle I went to a dormitory with twenty other guys.

I spent my working days in a workshop where benches
were piled high with scrapped carburettors. At these long
wooden benches we had the mindless job of stripping them
down. We took out the jets and floats and sorted the brass
and aluminium into separate piles. Even the fixed brass
inserts had to be removed and this sometimes meant smash-
ing them like cracked nuts.

The workshop overlooked the Solent. From my days at
the children's home I knew that on the other side of the
wall was a busy world of river traffic, of large channel
ferries and small sailing-boats. But the windows were too
high for any of these things to be seen from this room.
They were part of a world that no longer existed for me –
except on Sundays.

All the inmates had to go to chapel on Sundays. The
chapel was above the workshop so that from its windows
it was possible to see the river and its traffic. But it needed
courage. It was a bigger offence to look out of the window
than it was to talk, and being caught could mean a loss of
remission. So it had to be done slyly. A brief glimpse of
the sun on the blue water and of white sails made me
desperately want to be free. I used to curse the screws who
kept watch on us all the time.

It was at Gosport I first learnt to hate prison officers. I rarely met a decent one. Although to be fair, it was more noise than action. They were not as hard-hearted as the prison officers I later met in Wandsworth, or Chelmsford or on the Moor. I was beaten up only once by a screw while in detention.

But they have other ways of humiliating you. Cutting your hair is one of them. I had my first haircut the day after arriving at the centre. The barber was a Jekyll-and-Hyde screw with a poor sense of humour.

As I sat on a hard wooden chair in the centre of my cubicle, he walked round me once and grinned.

'How do you like your hair son?'

I grinned back, only dimly aware that the joke was on me.

'I'll have a Boston at the back. Square it off not too short. And sideboards down to here.' I drew a line with my finger an inch below my ear.'

'OK son. Let's see what I can do.'

The electric clippers were plugged in. He switched them on and I felt the vibrating blades at the back of my neck. Straight up he went with them, over the top leaving a broad band of closely shaved head – like a Mohican in reverse.

'Hey, what are you doing?' I stammered.

'Shu . . . t up!' He laughed loudly when he saw I wasn't pleased and then went on to lawnmower the rest of my head. In three days he was back to repeat the job, and in the first ten days I had three haircuts. Even now in my thirties I like to wear my hair long. To have it all off at seventeen was a shattering blow to my pride. Only because all the other inmates looked the same was I able to live with it.

Towards the end of my stay at Gosport I was put in charge of my dormitory. The screw who gave me the job made it clear he wasn't doing me any favours.

'I ain't done it 'cos I like you,' he said. 'Anything goes wrong and you get blamed for it.'

I didn't have to wait long to find out he meant it. Two nights after I got the job a couple of new inmates were sent to our dormitory. The way they rabbited to each other, they obviously came in together as friends. And from their girlish giggles I reckoned they were going to give me trouble.

Before lights went out there was often time for larking about, if the screw wasn't too near. Sometimes we would put our voices to the test with a singsong and there were always jokes to tell. But the rules were that when the lights were switched off the dormitory would go silent.

But these two new inmates didn't want to know the rules. My bed was half-way down the dormitory. One of the new guys was opposite and the other somewhere off to my right. They just kept talking and giggling, despite muffled threats from the rest of us.

The door opened suddenly. My friendly screw stood framed in the light from the corridor. He had been waiting outside.

'Out you come, Greenaway,' he commanded.

'Why me?' I protested.

'You're in charge and there's too much noise. Now out.'

In pyjamas and shoes I was marched to the gymnasium. I knew the routine. Every day it was the same. Only now it was night-time and the gym was empty. Bunny hops, press-ups, weight-lifting and to finish, running up and down rope netting. He made me go through the whole routine twice.

'Right, now outside.'

'Outside, in my pyjamas?' I swore at him under my breath.

'You heard. You've got six minutes to do a mile.'

When I got back, sweating, he made me stand in the corridor outside our dormitory. Although the sweat ran down my face and body, I soon began to shiver. The corridor was like an ice-box. He left me standing there for what seemed like hours. Everything was quiet now on the other side of the dormitory door. Eventually the screw returned, unlocked the door to let me back into the room. There was a grin on his face. He knew that it would take me a few minutes to get back to bed and that on the way I would have my revenge on the two guys who had got me into trouble. That night they learned the rules the hard way and in the morning they were quieter than usual.

Experiences like this one taught me a lot during my stay at Gosport. In just under three months I grew physically and I grew in cunning. I got to know and despise the screws and to understand something of how their minds worked. I learned how to defend myself and to get my own way with other inmates.

I had been given a short, sharp introduction to prison life. I left the detention centre in the autumn of 1964 with experiences that were to prove useful during the next seven years of violence and conflict with the law. From now on it was going to be increasingly difficult to lead a normal life. Not that I tried very hard.

5
HELL'S ANGELS

It was asking for trouble going back to the same hotel after leaving the detention centre. But again, it seemed the only thing to do. Before I was sent to Gosport the hotel boss had said in court that he would have me back afterwards. Things were different now though. I was a thief with a record and he held it against me. After the first couple of days it began to get really heavy.

The vibrations were made worse by two other people working at the hotel. One of them happened to be a guy I had worked with in my first job, at the reservoir, helping him to mix concrete. Here he was a still-room porter washing the silver and glass. We quickly became mates. The other guy was the head waiter, an Italian. He had an Italian bird living with him in the hotel.

Some of us lived in a chalet at the back of the hotel. Those of us who stayed there had no privacy. Through the paper-thin walls we could hear everything that was going on. It got up my nose the way the head waiter treated his bird, shouting at her and smacking her around. Me and my mate would have birds most nights but we never made the noise these two made.

As it was, there was plenty of aggro between the waiters and kitchen staff, mainly because the waiters got the tips and we didn't.

I'd only been back at the hotel a few days when my mate dropped a large urn used for making coffee. It had a glass inside which broke with a crash that brought the nosey head waiter rushing into the kitchen. He started swearing and blinding like it was his urn that had been broken. Not content with that he went and fetched the boss. He sacked my mate on the spot. It wasn't just the urn that did it. When it came to making a choice, an Italian head waiter was more valuable than a still-room porter.

It didn't worry the boss either that I gave a week's notice in protest. I offered to stay until he could find someone to take my place. The next morning he said he'd found someone. That's how keen he was on keeping me. Now I had no job. The cook at the hotel had a friend who was chef at a big holiday camp just along the coast at West Wittering. She persuaded him to take me on, helping in the kitchen. He wasn't keen but he agreed.

This was a big holiday camp needing lots of temporary workers. He couldn't afford to be fussy.

Some of the guys I teamed up with were ex-borstal boys. Working there was the nearest I had so far got to belonging to a gang. All the action was aimed at pulling the birds on holiday – a new bird every night if possible. A popular hunting-ground was a travelling fair that had been nearby most of the summer. It was a battleground as well, with lots of aggravation between us and the workers at the fair. We would often go down there team-handed, threatening to start a fight, but the truth was they were too tough and too experienced for us.

What finished the holiday camp for me was the thieving. There was a lot of it going on and it brought in the police. I'd only left the detention centre about a month before and I didn't like the law being that close. So I quit and joined the fair, working on the dodgems.

Working on a fair-ground as a casual cowboy was tough. There were two types of people working there: the fair people proper who owned the stalls and lived in glass-filled caravans that were more like palaces. And there were the casual workers like me who slept rough, perhaps with half a dozen others, in a caravan used mainly as a store-room. And the choice of company was limited. It sounds funny now but I couldn't understand then how so many ex-gaol-birds got jobs on the fair. I didn't think of myself like that.

The pay was miserable, about a pound a day. But an old lag showed me how to make up for it by twisting the customers. That wasn't thieving, of course. It was fair game short-changing mugs. I quickly learned how to make an extra five or six pounds a night. Most customers didn't bother to check their change. If they did, I argued with them and if they got too lippy I just got mad and hit them in the mouth.

It was then I learned to fight properly, putting the victim down to stay down. The first time was with a local guy, a straight citizen who had accused me of short-changing him. He wouldn't take a smack in the mouth as an answer so I knocked him down and walked away. Up till then, that was how I had always fought. But this guy was no chicken, he got up and jumped on my back. Although I could have handled it, several of the other fair-ground guys dragged him off me into the darkness behind one of the generators and beat him into the ground with sticks and boots until he couldn't get up.

Afterwards the most vicious of my new-found workmates gave me a lecture. 'When you hit them down, don't let them get up again. Put them down to stay there and if you have to, jump on them.'

From then on, that was the way I fought, and in the couple of months I spent with the fair it happened more than once.

The fair moved around a bit before it finished the season at Petersfield of all places. Again I was out of a job. No way was I going to go back home this time. The place would not have been big enough for us. My mother and stepfather wouldn't be any good for me and I hated their front. On the fair I'd got used to living rough, so for the first couple of nights I slept in the open. It was autumn and I would wake up wet with dew.

There was only one place around Petersfield where someone who dressed and smelt like me, and had no money, could get any digs. It was a transport café on the A3 London to Portsmouth road. Rumour had it that it was also a brothel and there were a couple of girls staying there who were a bit 'iffy'. I got my meals and somewhere to sleep in exchange for doing odd jobs about the place and keeping the lorry-park tidy.

About this time, I met up with some of my old mates again. One of them, Tojo, still had his motor bike and sidecar. It wasn't so much a sidecar as a plank of wood on a combo frame. Tojo was the one who had first shown me how to ride a bike and now, when we met up again, we'd often go screaming off to the coast with me riding pillion and acting the lunatic on every bend. He was a completely unscientific nutter. Riding pillion with him was like a trip on the wall of death.

I was with Tojo when I saw my first Hell's Angels. It was 1965 at the height of the sea-front riots, with greasers in large numbers battling it out with mods and rockers. One Saturday, Tojo and I headed for Brighton to get involved. We went as greasers, the ones with long hair and motor bikes, to do battle with the mods, who had short hair and scooters. As we rode onto the promenade, fights were going on all around us. The police were heavy on the ground especially at the pier head. Already the ambulances were carting off the injured and there wasn't a straight citizen anywhere in sight. The part we chose in the battle was to ride up and down the promenade with me lashing out at any mods who got close enough to us with a club I'd brought with me. Tojo then tried to run them down using our third wheel. By keeping flexible we did quite a bit of damage without getting caught ourselves.

In amongst the fighters was an odd crowd of guys doing their own bit of damage to any mods they could find. Like greasers, they had long hair but they kept themselves aloof from the rest of us. They wore sleeveless denim or leather jackets and heavily studded belts. On the back of every jacket was embroidered a skull and around it the words Hell's Angels. Although I'd heard of them and the violent worldwide brotherhood they belonged to, these were the first I'd ever seen. They were an exclusive bunch way above us and I was impressed by the way they were fighting. And later when I saw their bikes, shining and strange, like no other bikes I'd ever seen, it really blew my mind.

I stayed at the transport café only a couple of months but while I was there I met a bird I got rather stuck on. It was a bit more than a one-night stand. Soon I came under pressure to get steady work and a more respectable place to live. So I got a job with the Southern Electricity Board, putting up power lines. After a short while I moved to Leigh Park, a very big council estate on the edge of Portsmouth, to be nearer the Electricity Board's Depot. At last it looked as though I would have to put my wild days behind me and settle down.

The job was a good one. It was in the open air and although it meant being out in all kinds of weather, most of the time I liked it. So much so, in fact, that after a time as a labourer I became first a linesman's mate and then a linesman. I liked it even more when one day five gangs were brought together to work on a major repair of lines that had been brought down in a storm. The reason was my stepfather was working as a labourer for the Board and he was in one of the gangs. Through the pecking order, linesmen can tell labourers just what to do.

The weather was foul that day. I was strapped to a line pole with my mate. Below the pole my stepfather was working as a labourer. Up the pole we couldn't wear many clothes because we needed freedom to move and be able to reach the tools kept in belts round our waists. That day we were getting soaked but to me it didn't matter, just as long as I could order my stepfather to stay where he was at the bottom of the pole. Instead of letting him shelter under nearby trees when we didn't need him, I made him stay out in the open. I kept him there for several hours but he never complained. He knew for once I was his guv'nor.

Everything was going well with the job. I had no problems keeping my temper under control and I began to lead a proper life. I even took to wearing suits and carrying an umbrella like a real Jack-the-lad. But my violent temper hadn't gone; it was there just below the surface.

For more than a year I was OK. Things only began to go wrong when I was put on a newly-formed gang. A flash little linesman was made ganger in charge of us. He started right off by pushing his weight around. The very first day the gang was together working in the middle of nowhere he got us all together round him.

'Right,' he said in a loud menacing voice. 'Now that you are working for me you'll do what I say or else there is going to be trouble.'

It was all just heavy threats but he was nearer being right than he realized. Trouble followed quickly. A week or so later, four of us were putting up a wooden pole using long aluminium spikes which had handles at the bottom ends. As the other two in the gang spiked into the pole to lift it the last stage into position, my mate and I rested and chatted. It was the last pole of the day and we were behind time.

'Oi you, shut up and get on with the job!' It was the ganger getting uptight with me because it was late and he thought I was skiving.

'Who, me?'

'Yeah, you.'

I didn't like the aggressive way he spoke to me. He looked tough but I knew from what I had heard other linesmen say that he hadn't really got any bottle at all. Inside I was furious but I bit my lip and decided to wait. On the bus going home after work he always sat at the front near the door and facing the driver. That night, as I sat further back in the bus, the more I looked at him the more I wanted to take him apart.

The bus slowed down for us to get off. Just as he reached for the handle to pull himself up from his seat, I freaked out. Up the bus I flew. Grabbing the handle he was holding I butted him with my head. Behind me came a cheer.

'Get at him Brian!'

He stumbled and fell down the steps of the bus on to the pavement. The temper I had kept under control for so long had finally gone. Leaping on to him from the bus, I pummelled into him with all my strength until the blood started to flow from his nose and he began to cry. A grown man crying! I couldn't believe it.

'Leave me alone; leave me alone!' he pleaded, sobbing.

I couldn't handle that, so I just walked away down the road towards home thinking that I'd had my lot now and would be getting the sack in the morning. Maybe the boss didn't find out about the fight because I didn't lose my job. But the friction between me and the ganger from then on was pretty heavy. It could only be a matter of time before we came to blows again.

We managed to keep the peace for a couple of months. Then one day I was up a pole sagging in new cables. I sat belted in as I waited to give the signal that the lines were sagged the right amount. It sometimes took a couple of hours to get all the cables right, so I had made myself comfortable. From a long way off, the ganger saw me and must have thought I was crashed out asleep at the top of the pole. He must have been looking for an excuse to get even.

Reaching the bottom of the pole, he began ranting about me being asleep on the job. Then came a temptation I could not miss. Spread out on the crossbar of the pole were some of my tools. Amongst these was a hack-saw which only needed a push to send it hurtling down to the ground. It fell and missed him by just a couple of inches. He ran off screaming and shouting about me trying to kill him. Later that day I had him again and gave him a hammering for the second time. I tried to put him straight about what I was doing up the pole but he just argued back so I hit him and kept on hitting him, like I was back at the fair ground. This time the boss did come along. My violent temper lost me the only decent job I'd ever had.

6
THE GANG

Losing my job at the Electricity Board started me on the long downhill run that ended in Dartmoor. The next six years were to be the most vicious, desperate and self-destructive years of my life. Up till now every fight I had been in, every drug and drink I had experimented with was like nothing had happened in comparison.

From machine operator to fork-lift truck driver, I went quickly through one job and one factory after another. I was out of work more often than I was in. Each job was OK until I rowed with a boss or a workmate. Then, after an argument or fight, it was 'on your bike pal' and the factory door would shut behind me.

Drugs were partly to blame for my quick temper. From being cool, they could make me freak out at the smallest thing which annoyed me. I had played around with them ever since I was fifteen, perhaps even earlier, beginning in an easy way with the odd sleeper and purple heart. But now I was into smoking pot and dropping pills every day. It was mostly tranquillizers and pep pills. The psychedelic drugs came later. There was a pub in Portsmouth where pushers and junkies mixed with the bikers who used the place regularly. I was one of their clients.

But most evenings, and during the day when I wasn't working, I went to a café in Leigh Park used by a lot of local bikers. To begin with, it was the bikes more than the bikers that attracted me to the place. Mine was a 250 Royal

Enfield. Other guys had much bigger bikes and there were a couple of Vincent Black Shadows that I felt very envious about. I became more and more hooked on the power and excitement of going too fast on these machines, with the wind in my chest and rude signs to the world.

From the main road the café looked respectable enough. The slum department was through the back. It was here that the bikers and their birds met. Many of them belonged to a way-out gang called the Living Dead who used the café as their base when they weren't out terrifying citizens or looking for skinheads. There were also the ordinary bikers with straight jobs and not much bottle.

In that back room a counter filled almost the whole of one wall. Chairs were arranged around the other three and in one corner was a juke-box. After a session of drugs I would sometimes lie on the floor zonked out of my head with one ear pressed hard up against the speaker blaring out crazy music. In the evening the room would be tight with smelling, smoking and swearing bodies. In the day there were just a few of us. A small group of rebels who preferred to live by their wits, thieving and conning where they could rather than working.

It was these guys who were soon to form my own Hell's Angels gang. I remember them best as Pete the Animal, Fat Mick, Holes, Bert Dog, Ali and Crazy Jim and there were other names just as weird. To them I was the Tramp after an American Hell's Angel, Terry the Tramp. I had known most of them when I was still with the Electricity Board. Then they had been straight guys who only put on their bike leathers and faded jeans in the evenings. When I lost my job I began to change all that.

Because I talked tough and was always in the front when there was any action, they listened to me. Under my influence these guys became rebellious and anti-authority, ready without reason to run down a scooter-guy or kick a copper's head in. I used them to get back at the world I hated. Many of them became thieves and junkies. Six of them are now dead from drugs. Most of them went to prison and one is still a gang leader.

One of my earliest mates was Pete the Animal. He was average height, had dark hair and a gap in his teeth. We had first met working at the fair. We had learned to twist the customers together. He then joined the merchant navy. Now we met up again while he was home on leave. The rest of us would help him spend his money. Sometimes he didn't have enough to get back to his ship. After a while he didn't bother and he became one of us.

One weekend, wandering around the side-shows at a fair-ground in Southsea, Pete and I picked up two young girls. Mine was slim and pretty. Both she and her friend came from Leigh Park and, although they didn't look like it, they were both at school. That should have warned me off. There were plenty of birds around without getting caught with one who was under-age, but at the end of the day I fancied her.

We met again and she started coming to the café. Soon everybody there knew she was my bird. She was a nice kid and she began to mean a lot to me. As I said, she was pretty. And I liked her company too. She got on well with the other guys and was as eager as the rest of us to get our motor-bike club going. But we all knew it would never happen while we stayed at the café on the same turf as the Living Dead.

Our chance came when the Portsmouth Council opened a youth club just off the main drag in Leigh Park. It was a new building with its own youth leader. We reckoned that he needed members, so we left the café and the Living Dead and moved in, bringing our bikes, drugs and weapons with us. Almost straight away we turned it into a motor bike club. We called it the Nomads – still a long way from Hell's Angels. The youth leader was secretary and on the surface everything was respectable.

We started with around eighty members. Most of them were straights, the sort who insured their bikes and paid their road tax. But it was still the hard core that ran it and who caused most of the trouble. It didn't take long for the action to get really heavy. News about the club and about who was running it spread to other gangs, mostly scooter boys and skinheads. They would pay us regular visits and nearly every night there was trouble which ended in a fight. We always went to the club well tooled up.

The law was never far away. In case they busted the club, which they sometimes did, we had to be sure that no one inside was carrying any weapon. We also had to be sure that the weapons could be got at quickly if a rival gang turned up. So I took on the job of lifting all the tools from the guys as they came in. I knew who had got what and where it was hidden. Each evening I locked away a lethal armoury of studded belts, chains, knuckledusters and blades.

Some of the more deadly weapons we left at home. That included my sawn-off shot-gun which stayed in my bedroom unless it was really needed. One night it was. The trouble began when I was leaning against a Transit Van parked outside the club, talking to a group of mates. A couple of youngsters came round from the back of the building. One had a broken bottle in his hand and they were sparring around pretending to be fighting.

'Hey, you two!'

They both turned and stared at me when I called to them.

'What d'you want?' said the one with the bottle, very offhanded.

'Get rid of that bottle. If the law comes by they'll bust you for aggravation and the club as well. So pack it in.'

With a bottle in his hand he must have thought he could take me. He moved towards me, the bottle's jagged edge facing frontwards.

'Who do you think you are, pal?'

He got within five or six feet, jabbing at me with the broken bottle. I didn't scare that easy. Around my waist was a thick leather belt and on it were over two hundred pointed metal studs. I wore it fastened with only one clip so that it would come off with just one flick of my thumb. As this guy came at me with a stupid grin on his face I leapt up from the van. With the heavy belt I hit him twice across the body and it laid him down. He got up painfully, threatening he'd get someone on me, and walked off into the club with his mate.

I leant back on the van.

'Now, what was I saying?'

My mates appreciated the joke, and the confrontation was soon forgotten. But it wasn't over.

A couple of nights later, I was up at the counter inside the club. A voice called out to me across the crowded room.

'Hey, Brian, there's someone outside in a car wants to see you.'

The speaker was one of the odd Teds who came to the club sometimes. I knew when something was iffy and I could smell it this time. I turned to Fat Mick who was lounging nearby.

'Go and suss it out for me.'

He came back quickly to report. There were two guys sitting in a Mini a little way beyond the club car park. One was in the driving-seat and the other was in the back seat with the window taken out. A double-barrelled shot-gun pointed at the club door. This was the brother of the kid who had threatened to get on to me. The gun was going to blast me as I walked through the door.

When Mick came back with the news, I dived out of the back window of the club and raced home to get my sawn-off twelve-bore. If there was going to be a gun battle I wanted things to be even in my favour. When I got back, the car had gone. They had either lost their bottle or just got fed up with waiting. That was the sort of pace we lived at even during the early days of the motor-bike club. And when there was action, I was always in the front line.

About a year after we moved to the youth club, a few of us decided that it was time we started a proper Hell's Angels Club so that we could have an identity and take care of ourselves in an organized way. At a special meeting which packed the club I told everyone of our plans. No one was surprised when I was voted president. Bert Dog became my vice president and Fat Mick was made Lieutenant or Sergeant-at-Arms. That night the youth leader decided to keep well out of the way.

At that time there were more than eighty guys and birds coming to the club – a lot more than we could handle. Most of them weren't tough or ruthless enough to be Hell's Angels, even if they had wanted to be. So my first job as president was to get rid of two-thirds of them. That left us with nearly thirty to form the hard core. These were the nutters who I knew would do what I asked them to do, the ones I could take into action against rival clubs with a good chance of winning.

News went around about the new club. My girl's parents were very unhappy that she spent so much time after school with me and with the club. Things at her house got so heavy that she decided to do a runner with one of her school friends. One evening they turned up at the club, packed and ready to go.

When they told me what they were going to do I freaked out. It would make things worse for them and for the club and for me. Bringing them back made things a bit easier between me and her parents. They already knew what sort of relationship we were having. They didn't like it but it wasn't that uncommon around Leigh Park. The other girl's parents took a harder line and got the police involved.

When my name came up, they grilled the bird hard about my relationship with her friend. They were dead keen to get one over on me. So I got nicked for what I'd done and was given a six-months' suspended prison sentence. I was twenty-two. Until now I had only been to Petersfield Magistrates' Court, but this time it was the Hampshire Quarter Sessions in Winchester.

Three months later I was done for theft from a prepayment electricity meter. I was always short of money and most of what I had went on drugs or pot. If I didn't have a job, I relied on thieving, mostly bike parts, and on conning people – obtaining money by deception as my record sheet puts it. The time I opened the meter I was flat broke and hadn't got any change to keep the electricity on in the council house where I lived. I broke the lock, took out the money and fed some of it back into the meter to put the electricity on again.

Next day the meter man came and saw the busted lock. I got three years' probation for that. I was still free to make a nuisance at the club and my reputation grew. The law began putting on the pressure. I even got pulled in for things I hadn't done. If they turned up at my house I had an axe behind the door in case they tried to get rough. One copper in particular was a regular visitor from the CID. More than once I threatened to cut his head off if he put his foot over the doorstep.

One day he and his mate turned up at the house to question me about an attempted safe-cracking. I knew it had nothing to do with me so I agreed to go with them to the local police station, an ordinary semi on the estate. Here they grilled me until they finally realized I wasn't guilty and let me go. Shortly afterwards, the mates I'd left back at the house playing cards turned up team-handed at the station with petrol bombs, threatening to blow the place up if I wasn't released. It took them some time to be convinced that I wasn't still there.

Shortly after being put on probation I got done again as a long list of offences caught up with me: obtaining money by deception; wilful damage (I broke up a police cell); no driving licence; no insurance; obtaining property by deception. To these were added the previous charges and in June 1969, I got my first prison sentence – twelve months in Winchester.

7
LEIGH PARK CHAPTER

I had an easy time in Winchester prison. With one third off for good behaviour the clothes hanger had hardly stopped swinging by the time I hung my prison uniform up again. It was our local nick and several of my mates were in there already. We lived three–up—that's three in one cell. As president of a Hell's Angels gang I was the sort of daddy, so things went pretty well. I did get sore that no one from outside came to visit me. It made me determined not to have anything to do with the Hell's Angels crowd when I got out. But within a week of release I was back with them again. One reason was that I now had nowhere to live. Pete found me digs in Leigh Park with Jacky. She was, I guess, about ten years older than me and lived in a flat with her two sons aged eleven and fourteen.

She knew I had come out of nick but my record and past life didn't seem to bother her. I soon found she was the sort who would help anyone in trouble without worrying too much about what the neighbours thought, and they thought plenty. At first she let me stay for a week or so, until I found somewhere permanent. I'm sure she knew that I didn't look very hard. After a while she applied to the council for me to be a permanent lodger. Except for when I was in prison, I stayed with her for the next three years. She was better than a mother to me.

While I was in Winchester, the Hell's Angels club had folded up because there was no one to lead it. Most of the old gang drifted to the café or just used the youth club in the ordinary way. But the hard core were still together when I got out and I soon had them interested again. This time it would be the real thing, a proper chapter like the original Hell's Angels in America. It would be an exclusive family of people who worshipped their motor bikes.

The bike was the most important thing belonging to a Hell's Angel. It was his idol. He kept his bike so clean that every part from the saddle to the sump gleamed. He would strip it down on the dining-room table and often it was parked amongst the furniture in the living-room.

As well as being his idol, the bike was his altar. When a Hell's Angel wanted a chick to himself, the two of them would go through a sort of marriage ceremony. This took place across the bike. The president was the priest and the motor-bike manual was the bible. After the marriage the bird became his old lady and until he got tired of her no one else would touch her. The penalty was a busted head.

Once we got the chapter really organized there was no shortage of birds – ever. We even had crazy girls of fifteen or sixteen from the local high school queuing up to be mammas – birds prepared to jump on to anybody's bike and into anybody's bed. We treated them like nobodies but they thought it was a privilege to sleep around and be seen around with us.

We started the chapter with about twenty guys and their birds. It gradually grew to about fifty over the next two years. Not anyone could join, even if he did have a gleaming bike. In the end it was very hard to get in. The guy had to be a prospector first, and to prospect for our chapter he needed my agreement. That wasn't easy.

To get accepted the prospector had to show class by doing the sort of things that would make any straight citizen throw up. If he cooked a dead dog and ate it, that was showing class. And it was done. One guy in studded boots stomped across the bonnets and roofs of half a dozen cars parked outside a pub – sending paint and metal chips flying.

Because we made it so hard to get into the Hell's Angels it was always a close-knit family. If any one of our guys got done over we would not stop until we had found out who did it and went and put them down. One of the places this happened was Hayling Island. The Island and its beaches were near enough to Leigh Park for us to go there often.

Our usual spot was a roundabout on a busy road near the fair-ground. Here, under the bright street-lights, we would park our bikes and sit watching the birds go by. But this particular night we were there on business. A couple of our guys had been done over by skinheads from the Island and we had come down team-handed to find them. As soon as we crossed over to the Island we notched up a couple of them on our belts but these were not the ones we were looking for. We expected to find these at the fair. And we did.

We split up into two groups of about a dozen in each and, not long after, Fat Mick saw the two guys we were looking for chatting to some birds by a coconut shy. They saw us coming and ran. Mick and I went after them, leaving the rest to keep their eyes open for other skinheads and for the law. Mick didn't have much bottle, so I always tried to get him into fights to toughen him up. In the darkness on the edge of the fair was a coach and car park. The two skinheads made for it.

We soon overtook them and had them trapped between two buses. They fought back hard and dirty but they didn't have the tools. My guy soon went down. I had him against the radiator grill of a bus and my knuckledusters were having an effect on his face. With a blow to the head and my knee in his stomach he went down and hit his head hard on the bumper. He lay there unconscious, blood trickling from his torn face.

A little way off, the rest of our guys were doing battle

with a large number of skinheads who had turned up with
shot-guns looking for their mates.

Mick was having trouble with his guy. He could not put
him down and was beginning to get tired. I ran into the
guy from the back with my head down. Mick stepped out
of the way and left him to me. It wasn't that we believed
in fighting clean. It was common for six of us to kick the
hell out of one guy. But Mick was beat and my head under
the other guy's ribs had put him down so that I could
handle him on my own.

Before he had time to move I had put a heavy-studded
boot into his side. I stepped back to regain my balance. He
groaned and rolled over on his back. There was a look of
fear on his face that sent me coconuts. I leapt towards him
with both boots in the air and came down on his face. He
screamed into unconsciousness. My mates had been
avenged and we went back to Leigh Park feeling pleased
with ourselves. Into the bargain we had a new shot-gun
taken from the skinheads.

It was after coming out of Winchester that I started
taking morphine. The first time it was on the 'script' as a
pain-killer for a dental abscess. My local 'vet' had carelessly
over-prescribed these pain-killing tablets, so I began pump-
ing myself with them. To begin with they gave me a really
nice feeling but soon I was hooked. Before the prescribed
pills ran out I had made contact with a supplier in Portsmouth. He kept me going for several months.

Suddenly the supply dried up. I couldn't get any anywhere and I had to go into cold turkey until the craving
went. I spent three days in bed feeling like I was going to
die. One time my body would be in a hot sweat and then
it would be freezing cold. I began to shiver and tremble.
Every time I moved my head I vomited. Jacky didn't know
where I was at. The sight of a junky going through withdrawal symptoms was new to her. After two days she called
the doctor. He certainly knew where I was at but by the

time he came I was nearly through it so I didn't tell him anything.

Jacky asked no questions. She just looked after me, nursing me and cleaning up after me when I threw up. She got away with things no other bird could ever do. She even washed my originals – the jeans which are part of a Hell's Angels uniform and are never supposed to be washed. Like his colours embroidered into the back of his jacket, the stains of the grease, blood and excrement on his originals are all the outward marks of a real Hell's Angel. But she would just pick up the jeans with a pair of washing-tongs and drop them into her washing-machine. Anyone else doing that would have got carved up.

Even though we were rebels and always in trouble with the law we were still able to use the youth club. It wasn't only that the youth leader couldn't stop us. He was more interested in trying to get through to us than getting rid of us. We thought it was a big laugh and took advantage of him most of the time. The minister of a local church also came to the club sometimes. He dressed in ordinary trousers and a floral shirt. This was the time of Flower Power. He even wore beads at one time. Although we mocked him we got on OK together. In many ways he helped me a lot when I needed him.

In the ten months between coming out of Winchester and stabbing the two guys on Bognor front, I tangled with the law quite a few times. Three times I was back at court. Now it was Havant Magistrates' Court for theft, threatening behaviour and obscene language. I knew the law would do anything they could to get me nicked, and in return I never missed a chance to run them down or get one of them alone in a dark alley.

There was always a copper or two near the club when it shut at about half-past ten. One night Ali and I stayed behind with the club leader after the rest had gone. It was nearly eleven when we left the club by the back kitchen door and got on to my bike and rode out of the car park at the front of the club. The bike was an antique 600cc Panther combination. I'd only just bought it earlier in the day. I was keen to show it off, so we left in a cloud of dust as the rear wheel churned up the ground underneath it.

It was about a mile through the quiet housing estate to where Ali lived. The noise we made as the bike roared between council houses and grass verges attracted the attention of a copper walking on patrol. Because of the fights and the aggro that went on around the club, the law had taken to stopping anyone like us on sight. This copper was no different. About fifty yards ahead of us he stepped across the verge and into the road with his arm raised.

With my mate riding pillion I had to show class. I opened the throttle. I felt Ali's knees grip tight into the sides of the seat. The gap between us and the copper was closing. He leapt from the road on to the verge and the bike followed him, across the verge and the pavement. Only by jumping through a hedge into the darkness of someone's garden did he escape being hit by the side-car. Ali cheered and thumped me on the back. I'd done my bit for the rebel cause, so we went home.

As president of the Hell's Angels it was my job to keep everyone occupied. In the summer we would go for runs at the weekend. Leaving Friday night and coming back Sunday we would load up cans of beer, hot dogs and pills and go off into the country. We didn't sleep much. Mostly we would spend the time just talking, taking advantage of the birds or getting smashed. After trips out like this the journey home with fifty bikes in a line sometimes got a bit hairy.

It wasn't always easy thinking up places to go and there could be a lot of frustration especially if there wasn't much money to go round. Either the guys had been at work all week and at the weekend wanted to see some action, or they were high on drugs and were getting aggressive. It was a weekend like this that ended in me stabbing the two guys at Bognor. One after another my plans went wrong.

On the Friday evening the whole gang of about fifty of us turned out to bust up a school dance. Most of the time we spent slumped against the hall wall spinning coke bottles at high speed across the floor between the dancing feet. The dance finished early when the guy running it panicked because I drop-kicked a Ted who got in my way. He called the police. They were still looking for the guys who tried to kill one of their mates by running him down, so we decided to clear out. The next night we all headed for a youth club in Chichester. We drove through the town, weaving slowly in line and trying to run down anyone who got in our way.

The club was a total disaster; no place for action at all and everyone began to get really wound up. I was worried. My ego would be in trouble if I couldn't hold them together. Someone mentioned a barbeque on Bognor beach. It was a long ride and a lot of petrol but it would solve my problem, I thought. About half the guys split and went back to Leigh Park. The rest of us made our way over to Bognor to a barbeque that didn't happen and to a fight that led me straight into an eighteen-months' prison sentence, a sentence that was in no way like the easy ride I'd had in Winchester.

8
HARD STRETCH

The six long weeks between my arrest and sentence were spent on remand in Lewes prison, another local nick. Here, for the first and only time, I found myself on the right side of the screws. There was one in particular who treated me well. He was a principal officer. Because I hated being banged up during the day, he let me keep my door open. Before I left Lewes to begin my sentence I was able to repay him.

It happened when another guy on remand started having a verbal go at him. Annoyed by the row on the landing near my door I left my bunk and looked out. As I did, the guy brought out a blade he had hidden away. He lunged towards the screw. Instinctively I swung round the door post and wound into him as the screw stepped sideways. I grabbed the arm holding the knife. Other screws came running. They pinned him to the floor and took his knife away. Because I'd saved this screw from getting damaged I was in their good books for the rest of my stay.

It never happened that way in any other prison. I met very few screws that I could say anything good about. Even now the mental agony they caused me gets me uptight. After being sentenced at Lewes Assize I went straight to Wandsworth prison to wait for allocation. That was a terrible and evil place. It made Gosport Detention Centre seem like a holiday camp. In the short time I was there, my skin took on a prison pallor and my body and clothes the fetid prison smell.

The day-time in Wandsworth was spent sewing up grotty mail bags. We sat at a long wooden bench. One burly screw behind us and another each side rocked on their heels, daring us with their eyes to open our mouths. We were not allowed to talk and they would amuse themselves by seeing how many of us they could nick. If we did get nicked we could lose some of our remission. We went on Governor's report and anyone who argued would be in real trouble. The air in that prison was always full of tension. It was that sort of place.

Most prisons I have been in have the same routine for newly-arrived inmates. When you get there, you are taken from the police bus and banged up in a small cell not much bigger than a kennel. There are several of these cells which lead out into an office. Here you are weighed and measured. You strip naked and a screw searches you. He is looking for drugs under your armpits or a weapon strapped inside your thigh. Then come the questions.

'What's your name?'

'Brian Greenaway.'

'What are you in here for, Greenaway?'

You hesitate. There are always other prisoners in the room.

'It's written down there,' you answer, pointing to the paper the screw holds in his hand.

The screw's not put off. He repeats the question. So you tell him what he already knows, not for his benefit but for the other cons. If your crime is one that is not popular with the other prisoners, the news soon gets around. That's why sex cases get such bad treatment inside.

From the office a door and an alleyway lead to bathing-cubicles. After showering and drying you collect your prison kit: grey flannel trousers for best, a light and dark blue striped shirt which sounds OK but never fits, a grey jumper, a Beatle-style flannel jacket and a boiler suit for working in.

When you are dressed, you report to the governor, who tells you your release date, and the doctor, who asks you if you are fit.

'Yes, Sir,' you say, and that's your medical over.

From Wandsworth I was sent within a couple of weeks to Chelmsford maximum security prison. There I was petered up with an ex-Coldstream Guard. We were on the first floor. In the cell above us were three black guys. There were many blacks in Chelmsford and it was a very racial prison. Blacks and whites were always on the look-out for ways of getting to each other.

These three guys were into physical exercises. One day, not long after I had arrived, one of them was doing press-ups, using a chair to push away from. Each time he pushed up, two of the chairlegs came down with a bang on the cell floor. For up to fifteen minutes at a time there was a continuous bdonk, bdonk, bdonk, above my head.

After nearly two hours of getting bottled up, I finally freaked out.

'Shut up you black. . .'

From other cells on the landing came supporting cries. The banging stopped.

Early next morning as our cell doors were opened, I took my metal jug across the bridge. This linked the two sides of the landing around a centre well. On the other side was a recess in which there was a hot-water tap and sink. Chelmsford is the only prison I've been in with steaming hot water on tap for shaving.

As I came back across the bridge the three black guys from the cell above were coming down the landing. With them were three of their black friends. They had come down team-handed to sort me out. The so-called mate I shared my cell with put his head out of the door and, seeing them coming, banged up quickly. I was left outside to face them alone.

The nearest screw was at one end of the landing. If I waited where I was until my attackers reached me, I was going to get hurt. So, with the full jug in my hand, I charged at them showering them with hot water. I screamed and smashed into them, going crazy with the empty jug. I'd taken them by surprise, and by the time they had recovered, the screws had come running. I pleaded self defence and they believed me. All six guys got into hot water!

A further chance to get even came at midday. In front of me in the dinner queue was a freaky guy who I knew had a psychopathic hatred of blacks. I reckoned I was pretty good at psyching people up and I guessed how this guy would react if asked the right questions. Some way behind us in the queue were two of the guys from the upstairs cell. I began to wind the psychopath up and then asked the leading question.

'Is that right you're a spade lover?'

As I looked at him I pointed towards the back of the queue. He turned his head and saw the two blacks talking. It did the trick. His face went taut and pale with rage. He screamed out a stream of obscenities and the metal tray he was holding began to flay the air. A way through the queue opened up. He reached his victims and waded into them as I had done earlier in the day. But this time there was no plea of self defence. It was straightforward GBH. He got carted off and finished up in a mental prison.

That was my problem dealt with, I thought to myself, feeling that I had been very shrewd.

Life was going to get too hot in a cell so close to my new enemies. I couldn't count on my spineless cell-mate to help me. I got the screws to move me quickly. From the first floor I went downstairs to share the cell of an even stranger fellow. He was involved in black magic and called himself a high priest. He was a real professional who claimed he could call up demons.

From the beginning I was fascinated by his talk of the occult, of seances, telepathy and extra-sensory perception. And he was pleased to have a willing and captive listener. I became his pupil. He began to teach me about witchcraft and witches and their power over other people. I was especially interested in healing. I already knew a bit about the cures that could be made by calling on the right spirits. The mother of my Hell's Angel mate, Smithy, was a white witch and I had seen her in action with her crystal ball and tarot pack.

Most of what my new teacher showed me has now gone from my head. But I do remember that one day he started calling up a demon. I believed him when he said it was a dangerous and hard thing to do. He went down on his knees facing the cell door. As I watched from the edge of my bunk I was unable to take my eyes off his hunched-up form, shaking and trembling, and making low groaning noises. What he saw I don't know but it didn't last long and gradually he pulled himself out of his hypnotic state.

The most convincing experiment we carried out between us was in mental telepathy. By this time we were beginning to work closely together.

'Sometime soon,' he said to me one day, 'when we are in different parts of the prison, you'll get a message from me that there is a letter in the post for you.'

It would be a good test of telepathy and of ESP because I hardly ever got any mail. He worked as a cleaner on the prison landings above our cell and rarely left the wing. I worked in one of the workshops in the prison grounds several hundred yards away.

The message came four days later. Quite clearly as I worked at my bench I heard his voice.

'Your letter's arrived.'

And he was right. That day I got one of my rare letters from Jacky.

'Thanks for the message about the letter,' I said when I got back to the cell that evening.

'You got it then,' was all he said. To him it was no great event.

He continued to teach me for the next couple of months. I don't remember much of it now but he would tell me about the witches' meeting-places in London, of the covens and the sabbaths. I stayed deeply interested and excited, learning all the time – until he began to talk of sacrifices. Then, despite my violent past, I listened with horror as he told me what had happened to the child of an unmarried mother in a coven he'd belonged to.

The pregnant girl had been kept in hiding until the child had been born so that no one outside the coven would know. His description of how the child had been sacrificed freaked me out. Although I was hard and aggressive I could not think of a child being treated like that. I could be evil but not that evil. I had stabbed guys and kicked them blind and not cared. But to have an innocent child cut up and sacrificed to the devil was more than I could take. The lessons came to a quick end. I wanted only to get out of that cell for good.

I had one real mate in Chelmsford, an Irish guy named Billy. The first time I saw him he was standing ahead of me in the medicine queue. I was there for a tot of aspirin water – the regulation remedy for most things unless you're dying, then you got two. He was there on crutches.

I psyched him up as a loner but he seemed pleased enough to talk.

'How did you get your legs smashed up, mate?'

'A bus driver knocked me off my motor bike and broke them both.'

His voice was more full of hatred than conviction and his

story didn't come together, but when he mentioned motor bikes, we just had to be mates.

A few days after I had taken my last black magic lesson, Billy sidled up to me in the exercise yard.

'Get out of your cell,' he whispered, 'the guy you're in with is an informer. The London boys are going to do him over.'

I knew what that meant. I'd seen it happen. Not long after arriving at Chelmsford, walking through the cage tunnel from the cells to the football ground, I'd seen someone the London boys hadn't liked. He was staggering through the cage with his long, blond hair stained with blood. His face had been razored open and there was a knife wound in his stomach. It had happened in the open but the all-seeing television cameras hadn't stopped this guy being got at. After remembering that event I didn't need to hear Billy's warning twice.

Straight away I told the screws to get me another cell. And they did. It wasn't that I could order them about, they just knew what was going on. Not long after, the black magician was ghosted away to a wing kept for the special cases. All informers, rapists, and sex offenders get this treatment. They eat in their cells, exercise and work alone. Even then they are not safe. Other prisoners serve them their meals. It is not unheard of for the food to contain disinfectant or urine or broken glass. And if the screw isn't looking it will be spat in for good measure.

Drug-smuggling was common in Chelmsford – mostly pot for smoking. The psychedelic drugs were only just coming on to the scene. Although some of the prisoners were using them, the screws hadn't learned how to handle them. A couple of times I saw them taken by surprise. There was the time first thing in the morning when the cell doors were opened and from one cell came two prisoners on their hands and knees barking. They were on an LSD trip and thought they were dogs. Before the screw who opened the door could get away he'd been bitten in the leg.

It was Billy who introduced me to LSD and it was at Chelmsford that I had my first trip. We had become close friends and spent our free time together exercising on the prison rugby field.

As we walked around the field during exercise time, in full view of the television cameras high up on the prison building and the perimeter wall, Billy held out his open hand to me. In the palm was a tiny black speck.

'Want a trip?'

I couldn't believe it.

'I've got some microdot. Want some?'

Outside of prison I had been taking some sort of drug every day for a long time. Even here in prison I'd not been short of marijuana. But hallucinating pills like LSD microdots were something different. What better place to go on a trip into a psychedelic world than in the damp, evil and foul world of prison?

I gently pinched the small dot from the palm of Billy's hand and put it onto my tongue. At that moment the cameras must have been pointing in another direction. Our free time was over. I walked with the crowd back to the cells, banged up my door and threw myself on the bunk. The first of many trips had begun.

9
JESUS TRIP

By the time I was released from Chelmsford I was well into LSD. That much at least I have to blame on prison life. I was tripping nearly every day during the twelve months between my release and my final four-year sentence in January 1973 in the Moor. One tab would last anything up to eight hours and towards the end I was taking two at a time. I would go through ten trips of hell in an attempt to relive one good one.

My actions were becoming increasingly dangerous and irrational. I was back as president of the Hell's Angels and under my influence Pete and Smithy and several of the other guys were becoming junkies too. Every day was a day of violence. I still carried a knife and rolled-up bike chain. And I used them. More and more my shot-gun went with me when we were out looking for trouble.

None of us cared what drug-taking was doing to us or what a menace we were, tearing through busy high streets on our bikes. We just chewed the tiny black tablet and waited. If we escaped the severe stomach-cramp which sometimes came we would wander off into a strange psychedelic world of hallucinations. At times it could be very vivid. Other times there would be no sensation to begin with, just a tingling in the face, and then we'd be away.

On a trip anything became possible. Indoors the walls could breathe in and out. Plants printed on to the wall paper could begin to grow. On a trip I have watched maggots as thick as my little finger crawl from the pores on the back of my hand.

One drizzly day, in the middle of a trip, Smithy and I decided to call on a mate who had moved to a new house. We walked for a long time. The fine rain soaked through our clothes. Mine clung to me and I knew I would feel bad later. But at the time the effect of the drugs kept me feeling cosy and warm. We came near to where our mate lived, walking along on the opposite pavement. I started to cross the road between two cars parked a little way apart.

Out of the corner of my eye I saw a movement. Suddenly, the bonnet of the car to my left leapt open and growled. The boot of the car at the other side of me did the same thing, showing a giant set of white, pointed teeth. I was vividly reliving a television advert on road safety. Scared for just a moment, I lurched and stumbled what seemed like five hundred yards to the other side of the road.

I wasn't sure which house my mate lived in, but in the drizzle, one house glowed with an aura, like the sun was shining on it. That, I thought, must be the one. I pointed and Smithy followed me uncertainly up the path. We knocked on the front door. There was no answer. Walking round to the back of the house we heard a noise coming from a garden shed. Inside was our friend. One look at his eyes with their tiny pin-hole pupils and you'd know he was tripping.

But Gary was different. He didn't have to take drugs any more. Now he was on a permanent trip and had no need of them. Not long after we visited him he left home and began wandering the country, his mind completely blown.

We went inside the shed and closed the door.

'Wanna hear some music?' he asked, slowly and sleepily.

He didn't move. Quietly from nowhere came strange musical sounds that built up in volume and then died away again.

'Wow, man.'

We did not know that he had his foot on a radio volume-control. In our drugged state, the sounds came from another world and just blew our minds. We fled from the shed. Gary followed us and, laughing, went ahead of us into the house.

I settled comfortably on his living-room settee ready for another trip. As it began I felt myself going insane. I was faced with a million questions. A big see-through balloon was suspended in the air in front of me. Inside it, dozens of cubes danced and turned – round and round. Sometimes there was a question on the side of a cube. On others, letters formed to make a name. My mind was being torn to pieces by a rapid succession of problems that I couldn't answer.

Time passed slowly but I could see the minute hand on the wall clock going round. In an armchair to my right, Smithy was going through the horrors. He was having a bad trip. His mouth kept opening and closing but no sound came out. His eyes rolled in their sockets, searching for something. Gary was perched on top of a child's rocking-chair, moving backwards and forwards. Under one of the rockers he had placed a musical box which began to play each time he rocked forward and stopped again when he rocked back.

As I looked back at Smithy, I had a powerful feeling that he was my brother and that I loved him. Then in a moment of clear thinking I began to feel guilty because it was me who had made him into a junky. The hallucinations began again.

A white figure was standing in front of me. Not blinding white but clean and pure and good. The face had deep blue eyes which took all my attention. We began a conversation. It was the sort of tripping conversation where half the questions and half the replies are left unsaid because there is an understanding at a deeper level. Each person can understand the other's mind.

'You're not who I think you are.'

'Yes I am.'

'No, you can't be.'

I knew nothing about God except that he was good and pure and holy and lived on a cloud way up in heaven. There was no way him and me were going to get it together and then, suddenly, he was there on my trip. We were talking and understanding each other.

The figure in white pointed to a marijuana plant growing in a pot on the window-sill. Slowly, I turned to see where he was pointing and then back again to look directly into his eyes. He was still there.

'See that plant?' he asked. 'If I pinch out the buds at the end of the branches I can make it grow the way I want it to grow. If I leave it then it will grow wild and there will be no fruit.'

At that moment I believed God was speaking to me. Although I didn't understand the full depth of what he was saying, he was on my trip.

All this happened four months after I left Chelmsford. In the evening I went home and told my landlady, Jacky.

I was very excited. 'I've seen God! I've seen God!'

Calmly she asked. 'Were you on drugs?'

I had to admit I was. For her, no further explanation was necessary. The illusion I had was gone. Even today I cannot explain what really happened on that trip but Jacky and I were to talk about it again three years later and both see things in a new way.

Slowly, the strain of spending up to eight hours a day tripping pulled my mind apart. I was becoming a mental wreck, unpredictable and just as likely to turn against my mates as against my enemies. I was still going with the girl from Leigh Park. On our weekend gang trips out into the country she would ride in the van we used for carting the food and the gear.

We spent one weekend in a ruined farm building several

fields away from any road. It was late summer and we'd brought a coal brazier to keep us warm. There were a couple of hundred bread rolls with cheese and sausages and a dozen gallon cans of lager and beer. This was mixed with a home beer brew. On the Saturday evening we huddled within the walls of the building, keeping warm by the fire and passing cans of drink from mouth to mouth.

Several of the guys began tripping. Something was wrong. These guys weren't junkies. Someone was dropping pills into the drink. I might have thought it a good joke if it hadn't been for my girl. She didn't drink much but was joining in now as the cans went round. Supposing she swallowed a pill?

I freaked out. Pete had been acting the clown as he usually did. There was a grin on his face like he was enjoying a private joke. It must be him popping the pills.

'Pete!' I roared. 'Are you dropping pills in the drinks?'

His grin broadened and then, as my temper flared, it died away.

I'd lynch him, the filthy swine.

In my drunken state I staggered to the van to get a tow-rope. I would string him up in a nearby tree. An argument was going on behind me. When I got back, Pete was in the middle of a fight. Another guy had started to take him apart while I'd been getting the rope. Pete was badly hurt and lay on the ground with his face gashed and bleeding. The sight of him cooled me down and I dropped the rope. I was glad he had got hurt. He may have been my best mate but he had done me a wrong.

I was beginning to distrust even my closest friends and I suspected they were growing tired of me. They were getting less willing to be led as I became more violent and paranoid. My mind was going out of gear and I knew it was happening. At times I began to get frightened. I lost interest in sleep and would spend the night-hours wandering alone through the streets of the housing estate.

I'd been out of prison nearly six months when one day I found myself in the doctor's surgery. I don't know how I got there or why I had gone. Smithy was in the waiting-room. It must have been clear to the doctor that I had been tripping.

'How long have you been on drugs?'

That was the first question I remember. Then for nearly an hour he pumped me with questions about drug-taking. Warning me, threatening me, and trying to persuade me to kick it. I could hear the people coughing and sneezing in the waiting-room getting more and more impatient. He made them wait as he tried to make me face reality. There was a drug rehabilitation centre in Portsmouth. I should go there for treatment, he said. He would give me a letter to take. I left with his warning ringing in my ears.

'If you don't stop taking drugs you will be dead in three months.'

If I didn't die from drug-taking I would get killed doing something stupid under its influence. He was only confirming what my psychiatrist in Chelmsford prison had told me. I was a psychopath with suicidal tendencies. I went home depressed and in my room I cried my eyes out. He was right in everything he said but I could see no reason to change my life. I saw no way that I was going to be able to break from the way I was living.

The one ray of hope was the Alpha Trust which ran the drug rehabilitation centre in Portsmouth recommended by my doctor. I had heard reports from my mates about this place. How you had to beg and crawl to get in and how if you did something wrong they shaved one side of your head or made you walk around the place wearing a big placard, 'I'm a naughty boy'. But I felt I had to do something. When I could think clearly, I didn't really want to die.

A month after meeting the doctor I packed my cases and persuaded Pete and Smithy and some of the other guys to go down with me to Alpha House. I was going to give it a try. We loaded the cases into a van I'd got hold of and started out. But we never made it. The traffic was crawling into Portsmouth City centre. From a line of parked cars alongside of us, a citizen driving an elderly Prefect pulled out in front. He had the room but I didn't let people do that sort of thing to me. I put my foot lightly on the accelerator. There was a tearing of metal as the van pulled off the car's front wing.

The guy made it clear that he wasn't happy about what I had done. The line of traffic ahead moved off and I pulled away. Then it stopped again a few yards further up and this time we were stuck. A panting Prefect-driver caught up with us and started raving through the side-window. I raved back even more colourfully but he wasn't put off. His shouting attracted a crowd and the crowd attracted a cop on a motor bike. He made us pull over to the kerb and get out of the van. We were in trouble. The van wasn't legal – no tax or insurance.

The copper didn't recognize us so we were all able to give false names and addresses. I remember mine was Alistair Crowley, the occultist. While Pete and Smithy were being questioned at one end of the van I backed off into the crowd and did a runner. I dodged in and out of shop doorways until I felt safe. Then I walked quickly towards the city centre the distance of a couple of bus stops. I got on a Leigh Park bus which brought me back past the parked van and crunched car. My mates, the car driver and the cop were all gone. My guys must have been booked, I thought.

Back at Leigh Park, I phoned my solicitor, telling him what had happened. I need not have worried. Shortly after, the guys came to the house. Like me they had done a runner and afterwards had gone back to pick up the van with the cases and bring it back to Leigh Park. I also phoned Alpha House telling them I wasn't going to make it. I never really believed that I would anyway. It was going to take more than the advice of a doctor to make me kick my bad habits.

10
FOUR YEARS

The summer of 1972 turned to autumn. My twenty-sixth birthday came and went and the three months my doctor had given me to live were nearly up. I'd been lucky to get this far but in the state I was in I couldn't hold out much longer. My psychopathic hatred for anyone outside the chapter grew daily. Even inside, friendships were beginning to wear thin. But I was still president. The spirit of brotherhood that we had started with hadn't completely gone. There was honour still to be defended even amongst our gang of thieves.

Since the time we moved into the council youth club three years ago we had kept up our love-hate relationship with the Living Dead at the local café. We'd had our fights but we learned to tolerate each other. Now they even came along with us on our weekend runs into the country.

One September evening a guy from the Living Dead arrived at the flat. He was on crutches and his face was badly bruised. He said six guys dressed up as Hell's Angels had attacked him and left him with a broken leg.

What was I going to do about it?

I didn't need much of an excuse to go on a revenge mission to sort out any gang that set itself up to rival us. And he knew it. From what he told me I knew they must have been a bunch of Honda freaks belonging to a Gosport motor-bike gang. With their plastic jackets and hand-painted colours on their backs they had been going around giving proper Hell's Angels a bad name.

I made a few phone calls to fetch out the others and then went to collect the van. The Living Dead guy hobbled along after me. With him and a van full of tooled-up Hell's Angels, plus a couple of bikes and a car load, about thirty of us set out to find the gang. I was driving – not too well because I was still having a trip that had started earlier in the day. It was a long drive to Gosport. We stopped at a café on the way. Here I dropped my second tab, so that by the time we reached Gosport I was pretty high. Some of the other guys were tripping too. Along the main drag into Gosport, cars and buses were coming past us at about 150 miles an hour and I could smell burning rubber all the time.

With five of us squeezed into the front seat of the Transit van, driving was even more difficult. We made it to Gosport and started a slow search of the town for any gang members who were around. It took us a long time. Although it was light when we first got there it was now beginning to get dark. Pete, sitting next to me, was the first to see anyone.

'There they are.' He'd seen six of them talking together outside a pub. More were visible inside, through a half-open door.

The guys on the bikes in front of us had also seen them and had parked. I pulled the van up sharply. The doors burst open and the other guys in the van were out and across the road, creating chaos with the evening traffic. We weren't going to let anybody get away.

I pulled the van into the kerb opposite the pub. A guy and his bird saying good-night leapt for their lives as I swung in to the edge of the road and collided with the bike the girl had been sitting on. I had arrived. I dived across the road into the hysterical and blurred heap of fighting bodies.

The Gosport guys must have been outnumbered at least

two to one. They started off by fighting fair. But we went in like animals, using all the wood and metal we had brought with us. By the time I got into the action, most of the damage had been done. One Gosport guy who had come out of the pub on crutches was lying in the gutter with bad head injuries – it turned out to be a fractured skull. One of his mates had picked up a crutch to defend himself.

'What's your game, mate?' I said, as I moved towards him with my rounders bat swinging.

'I'm just here to keep the peace,' he said lamely, putting up the crutch as a shield to defend himself.

For a brief moment I turned my head away, distracted by a body that came staggering past me. As I looked back, the crutch was coming down fast at me. My left arm went up to soften the blow as the crutch landed heavily across my shoulder. My right arm followed, bringing up the rounders bat to give a hard smack alongside the ear of the guy wielding the crutch.

'Well take a piece of that!' I laughed callously at my own joke.

The guy fell at my feet with a split down his face. For good measure I put the boot in but he was out too cold to feel it. In a few brief minutes six or seven Gosport guys were spread across the pavement and gutter, badly hurt. We'd had our revenge and now we had to get out quickly before the law arrived and before they would block the only main road out of Gosport. Someone had probably phoned them already.

The journey back to Leigh Park was a fight to keep it all together. Lights from the street lamps and passing buses came by like a storm of meteorites. The psychedelic effect of the LSD had been heightened by the fighting and I had a violent pain across my left shoulder. Through the front of the van the view was like a wide-screen cinema. As we reached the edge of Gosport a roundabout came up. There was no slowing down. We broadsided it, the van swaying dangerously to one side. A lamp post slid by. Our youngest recruit, sitting nearest the door, went pale.

'That was close, Brian.' He was losing his bottle but tried hard to play it cool.

The rest of us thought it was a good joke. We were high and to me at least it wouldn't have mattered if we'd all got wasted. Although we had got away from the scene of the fighting I knew the law would catch up with us. We'd done too much damage to get away with it.

Sure enough, our van had been recognized and so had I. Within a few days the law came looking around the estate. They caught up with me at the local café. It began when two young cops I didn't know turned up asking questions while several of us were there one evening. Through the back of the café came the message.

'The pigs are here.'

I looked cautiously round the door. These two I could handle. They were a couple of office types.

'Don't let's wait for them to come snooping in the back here. We'll go out after them.'

No one else moved. The fight in Gosport had been too much. They were getting tired of me and of the trouble I kept leading them into. I'd gone too far this time. They probably knew we would get picked up. For the sake of my ego I had to front these cops out alone. I didn't need anyone's help anyway. I walked through the café and out on to the pavement to meet them.

'I'm Greenaway. You looking for me?'

My approach took them by surprise but they weren't going to miss this chance.

'Get into the car, Greenaway.'

I knew better than to do that. I'd learnt the hard way what happens once you are inside a two-door panda car. You stand no chance. We went instead round the side of the café. After a few questions we began to argue. Then came the finger-poking bit. Until then I'd played it cool but this made me freak out. I grabbed the tunic of the guy who was asking all the questions and told him what I thought of the pigs. In another minute he would be on the floor.

At that moment, another police car arrived. Its doors opened and out rushed four local cops. These were the real thing – big, mean guys. I knew from past experience just how they could behave. I'd already had five front teeth kicked out by one of them and there were still a few scores they had to settle with me.

'Any trouble, Greenaway?'

'No trouble at all.'

For all my front I was beginning to lose my bottle. This time I got into the car when they leaned on me. My mates had all stood me up so I didn't have much option. Soon I was back at the police station being questioned.

It turned out that of all the guys who took part in the revenge raid, I was the only one to be positively identified. Five others including Pete got picked up a few days later on circumstantial evidence and we all got charged with causing an affray.

It didn't surprise me when none of us got bail. We were sent on remand to Winchester. It shouldn't have been too bad. We were all together in one wing away from the convicted prisoners. We wore our own clothes and could spend our money in the canteen. But we couldn't have gone at a worse time. Shortly after the six of us arrived, another six Hell's Angels came in on remand for raping an RAF girl in Aldershot. And then there was a young girl raped in Southampton by six more. By the time all eighteen of us were banged up together, three-up in one wing, Hell's Angels were very unpopular amongst the screws. And because I was the only president, I got leaned on the heaviest. If there was any trouble it was me the screws picked on. In return we gave them plenty.

About the time we were on remand, riots were going on

in other prisons and the screws here in Winchester were nervous. We did our best to make them that way. Our favourite game was to play tunes on the call bells in our cells. Not only did these ring when the button was pressed, but a flap with a number on it dropped down outside the cell. This was to let the screw on duty know which cell-bell rang.

One lunch-time I was ringing the bell in my cell because I wanted to be let out to the toilet. I'd been banged up with two other guys for most of the morning. Two screws came to see what I wanted. When they told me I would have to wait I started ringing the bell over and over again. From other cells on the wing came a chorus of bell-ringing.

The screws didn't like it. They came back and nicked me. There was a limit to the bad time they could give a guy on remand. If things got really bad, it would be down to the punishment cell. This was a damp, miserable rabbit-hutch below the main cells and kept for trouble-makers. I've spent up to four hours at a stretch in one. And this is where they took me now.

Before they threw me into the punishment cell I managed to knock off one of the screw's hat. The next thing I expected was a mattress to come flying into the cell with a team of screws on the other side. It didn't happen this time but it was a favourite trick if they wanted to show anyone in the punishment cell who was boss.

There was one screw in particular I managed to rub up the wrong way. He was a little guy who spent most of his energy shouting his mouth off at the prisoners. I gave him a lot of stick because he had a speech impediment – like his mouth was full of soap bubbles.

'Schlop out,' he would shout when the time came each morning to empty the slop buckets.

He was a natural butt for my twisted humour.

I used to mimic his speech when I got the chance. It used to send him bananas. This only encouraged the other guys to join in.

I spent nearly three months on remand, coming back to court each week to be remanded for another seven days while the police put their case together and got their statements. On 23 January 1973, I was sentenced to four years' imprisonment. Three years were for causing an affray, unlawful wounding and carrying an offensive weapon. Six months was added for driving while disqualified and the six months' suspended sentence I'd got earlier in the year for not having a driving licence was taken into account.

Pete got eighteen months and the other four guys got suspended sentences plus heavy fines. My sentence made me really mad. Why had I got so much more than the other guys? And what about the others in the fight who hadn't even been nicked? I asked my solicitor if I could appeal. He went and got the advice of the barrister who had defended me in court.

'Not the faintest chance of a successful appeal.' That was his verdict.

It wasn't just the fight which had brought me such a heavy sentence. Driving while disqualified and heavily under the influence of drugs went hard against me. But mostly it was my dreadful past record. It was, he said, as bad as it possibly could be.

He reckoned Pete's eighteen-months' sentence was too light and he hinted that if I appealed I could lose some of my remission. My only alternative to prison was to be detained at Alpha House under the Mental Health Act. But the judge and the guy running the centre had already decided against that idea. . .

While I was on remand I had been seeing two psychiatrists. They both reckoned I was hell-bent on self-destruction and too violent to be detained.

So after a few days back at Winchester, I found myself locked into a prison coach and travelling west across the bleakness of Dartmoor to Princetown and a new life.

11
THE MOOR

Eight handcuffed convicts left Winchester in the prison coach that took me to the Moor. Six guys were dropped off at other prisons on the way down. The journey began as an ego trip. I knew I was going to the real con's prison. They didn't have softees in the Moor. For the last part of the journey from Exeter to Princetown not much was said. I did not join in the screws' conversation but stared out between the horizontal bars of my window at the passing view.

From Mortonhamstead the winter scene became suddenly desolate. As the road went up, my spirits began to sink. It was late afternoon and the light was fading when the outer gates of the prison closed behind us. We waited as a screw at the gatehouse checked our papers handed in by the coach driver.

'OK,' he shouted, and the inner gates swung open.

Through the front windows of the coach I saw a scene like no other prison I'd ever been in. It wasn't the usual building with wings radiating out from a hub like the spokes of a wheel. Instead a number of separate black granite buildings were scattered around a vast open space – some connected by covered walkways.

Inside the high perimeter fence ran a wide roadway patrolled by dogs and their handlers. And inside that was an equally high wire fence. At intervals powerful floodlights mounted high up on poles were just coming on. No part of the ground escaped their penetrating light.

As we entered the prison grounds the coach stopped to let a column of prisoners past. It was a working-party returning to their cells. A dozen hardened faces, scarred with the evil of the place that was to be my new home, looked up at us. I could read contempt and derision in their eyes. From the middle of the column one con cried out, jeering at us and pointing a finger. He looked as if he were insane. Others joined in the fun until a guard from the back moved forwards to shut them up.

Outwardly my front went up and I stared back with cruel contempt. But inwardly I wanted to break through the bars of my window and tear this guy's throat out. I watched the column get smaller as the bus pulled away. Questions flashed across my mind. How long had he been in here? Would I ever freak out like him at the sight of a new prisoner coming in? For the first time I felt fear. This was no ordinary prison. I sensed it was an evil place. This is it, I thought. I was trapped. I started to shake.

Even after getting off the coach and being marched to reception I was shaking. I answered the screw's questions with a stutter. I couldn't get my mind together and had to pause to think before answering. There was more than just a high granite wall separating me from the outside world. This was a recidivist's prison. The cons just kept coming back. There was no real escape. My brain was done in and I was going mad.

From reception I was taken straight to my cell. In the Moor each prisoner had his own cell. It was the first time I hadn't been petered up with another prisoner. The next day I had to go through the farce of meeting the reception board. One part of the prison had been made into offices for the Governor, doctor, chaplain and welfare officer.

The Governor's office was two cells knocked into one. A hand-rail divided the two halves. Incoming prisoners on the left and discharged prisoners on the right. A white line was painted several feet in front of the Governor's desk. Two screws stood with their heels on the line and their backs to him, facing the door.

Left, right, left, right. I marched through the door from the waiting-room as my name was called. I came to a halt between the two screws who stood ready to protect their boss in case I should freak out and go for him. No fear of that. I'd learned in other prisons to treat the most hated Governor with respect.

'Greenaway 278431, Sir.'

'Your earliest release date is so-and-so.'

'Yes, Sir.' My answer came automatically. I wasn't really listening.

Then it was about turn and left, right, left, right, out through the same door. My interview with the Governor was over.

It was the same with the doctor.

'Greenaway 278431.'

'Everything all right, Greenaway?'

'Yes, Sir.'

'Right, get out.'

That was my medical. All of it.

With the chaplain, the routine was slightly different. In his office I was allowed to sit down, and we were alone. As he talked he pushed a tin of tobacco across his desk.

'Roll yourself a fag, lad.'

In prison tobacco could buy almost anything. With just half an ounce a week as the ration, rolled cigarettes were usually thinner than matchsticks. Any offer of free tobacco was taken advantage of. I took the tin and rolled the biggest cigarette that could be got inside one piece of fag paper. A nice guy this chaplain. But I soon psyched him out. He was trying to buy my co-operation – the one thing tobacco won't buy.

He turned out to be a swearing drunkard who even the

screws hated. No way was this so-called man of God a Christian and more than once I could have cheerfully strangled him. He was the most evil man I had ever met and I've met quite a few. He made no effort to help anyone he didn't happen to like. He stayed at the Moor for about a year after I came. Then, around Christmas time, during a concert when all the cons and the screws were together, he announced he was leaving. He found out then just how popular he was. The cheer that went up nearly raised the roof.

There was one other guy on the reception board I met that day – the welfare officer. He was a probation officer working inside the prison.

'Sit down, Brian.'

At least his was a friendly face. I began to relax.

'What are you going to do when you get out?'

He must have made a mistake.

'I've only just come in,' I explained.

'Yes, I know. But we've got to make plans so that you've something to go to when you get out.'

This blew my mind. I'd met this nonsense before. I moved to the edge of my chair.

'Listen, pal. Last time I was in nick you guys talked about what I should do when I got out. You fixed it all up for me. Go to the probation office in Portsmouth, you said. It's all sussed out. We've got somewhere for you to stay. When I got there they'd never heard of me. So don't give me that waffle about trying to help.'

He knew all about that, he said. That was why he wanted to sort out my future now.

I didn't want to know. It was time to put on the front again. This time with a threat.

'If you ever stick your face near me again, I'll kill you,' I said, and walked out of his room.

My first couple of months in the Moor were spent working in the TV shop. Day after day I put metal sleeves on to the ends of coloured wires. We were paid according to how many we assembled. The rate was set by the fastest worker. Because there was one guy who flashed through the work, the rest of us didn't get much. If I did this for much longer I was going to crack up. I had to screw my loaf and find a way out of this job.

My chance came when I applied for a place on a building course. It was supposed to be for a City and Guilds Certificate but no one was encouraged to take exams. I did learn a lot though – about bricklaying, and putting up roofs and laying drains. Our civilian instructor even got me reading a theodolite for surveying.

There were eight cons on the course; a Scot I got on well with, five Taffies who kept to themselves and a cockney who got on my nerves always shouting his mouth off – until one day, when the screws weren't looking, I hit him with a piece of four-by-two.

At the end of the three-months' course I was lucky enough to be put into the prison works department. Here was an elite bunch of guys who worked with the screws and civilians to maintain the prison buildings. I was paired up with an electrician, a thin, unhealthy civilian who seemed to get a kick out of having a Hell's Angel president working with him. We got on well together.

One wing of the prison was being ripped out and we had the job of rewiring it. Sometimes I worked on the floodlights in the grounds if they went wrong. This meant going up in the tower truck to fix them. From a height I could see over the wall and across the moor. In the distance would be parked cars and tourists. Occasionally I saw the glint of light from a pair of field glasses. It freaked me to think that we were a tourist attraction. I must have spent too long looking over the wall one day because after that I didn't get the chance to use the crane again.

In the Moor there were so many rules. And there was always a screw around to catch you if you broke any. It didn't pay to get on the wrong side of a screw. He could make your life a misery. You soon got your cards marked if you did anything he didn't like. I found that out early on. Each evening after tea we were unlocked from our cells to slop out. Most of us then went down for a time of recreation. There was one guy I used to play table tennis with in the evening – to begin with. Then one evening on the way back to my cell a screw stopped me.

'Do you know who you've been playing with?'

I shrugged my shoulders. All I knew was he could play table tennis. I didn't go round asking guys what they were in for.

'He's a nonce.' That's prison slang for a rapist.

That shook me. I knew that all sex cases got a bad time in prison, both from the screws and from other prisoners but usually they finished up in a separate wing out of harm's way. This guy was well built and had obviously learned to take care of himself. The screws were trying a different way of getting at him by warning everybody off.

Now I'd got a problem. Either I stopped playing with this guy or I was going to have the screws on my back. The next evening I chanced another game. That was enough. The same screw was there watching again. I could see he thought I was trying to wind him up. Given the excuse he would have come steaming into me. Sooner or later, either I would have to take him apart, then I'd never get out of prison, or he would find some way for me to lose my remission.

The next evening after slopping out I banged myself up in my cell. And that's the way it was for the next couple of months, until one evening my landing screw asked me why I never went downstairs for recreation.

'I've got you down on my record as unsociable,' he told me.

'That's a joke. If I go downstairs I'm mixing with undesirables. If I stay in my cell I'm being unsociable. I can't win either way.'

I was going to stay in my cell and they could put what they liked on my records. My attitude towards other people wasn't helped by the fact that I was still suffering the effects of taking LSD every day in the months before my arrest. Although there were no physical withdrawal symptoms with LSD and the mental craving soon went, I now had no way of escaping when I got depressed. I had to face the hard realities of life.

Banged up in my cell for hours I had too much time to think. How did I fit into this crazy world where the only news was bad news? Maybe it was only me that was crazy and I'd really blown my mind. I thought of mates of mine who were doing Queen's pleasure for murder. It might as well be me. What about the times I'd terrorized a pub-load of people with a shot-gun? Why hadn't I blown someone's head off? I had knifed and blinded guys. Over and over again I remembered that I had been rejected by my family. It was a scar that never healed.

All this thinking made me bitter. It also made me desperate – so desperate that I began looking around for someone to help me. I asked to see the prison psychiatrist. Getting to see her wasn't that easy. First you asked, then you begged and finally you pleaded. By the time I got my first interview I was getting suicidal. If she couldn't help me then I was in real trouble.

As I poured out my problems and frustrations, as I told her the way I felt about the screws, she just sat in her chair and listened. She didn't argue with me and rarely spoke. If she did it was only to ask another question. I desperately wanted it to work but inside I knew there was no answer for me in psychiatry. It was no more than a badly needed safety valve.

Back in my cell after each session the same old question would come back to me. What was the meaning of it all?

Self-pity must have begun to show on my face. As I was being marched to a psyching session one day the screw who was taking me got mad.

'You make me sick, Greenaway, always screaming out for help. Why don't you try helping yourself for a change?'

Outwardly I blanked him. I would not let him know what I thought of his advice. And inwardly I was calling him a rat. That evening, like most evenings, I spent in my cell. And like most evenings, everything that had happened during the day came back to me. Uppermost in my mind was another wasted session with the psychiatrist.

Then I remembered the chance remark of the screw.

'Why don't you help yourself for a change?'

If only I could.

My mind flashed back to when I was first in trouble with the law as a lad. The probation officer had said much the same thing to me then. He was right and the screw was right and I knew it. But how? I was just an ignorant yobbo. What could I do to help myself?

12
THE YELLOW BOOK

I'd been in the Moor six months before I saw the welfare officer, Terry Scarborough, again. After our first confrontation he must have believed me when I threatened to kill him. Perhaps he'd had problems thinking out a way of getting through to me. One dinner-time at the beginning of August he came up to my cell. At the sight of him through the opening in the door I began to bottle up. I still had it in for him but the fight had gone out of me. I let him come in and he sat down. It was a few moments before he spoke.

'You don't get any visitors, do you?'

I shook my head.

'Who'd come all the way from Pompey just to see me?'

'I can get you a visitor if you want one.'

He told me about Malcolm Goodman, a farmer friend of his whose son sold motor bikes. He knew that as a Hell's Angel I must be a bike fanatic. Strangely, bikes didn't seem to interest me any more. It was going to be at least two years before I could see one close up again. And the way I felt it might be never. I had more serious things on my mind.

'OK,' I agreed after a long pause. 'I'd like someone to come to see me. But I want to talk about God.'

He must have had some strange requests in his time but I could see from his face that this one had really knocked him back. Why should a con with my record ask for such a thing? I didn't even know whether he believed in God. He muttered that he would arrange it – then left the cell.

Even I was surprised at the way my request had come out. Admittedly, I had always believed in God. I may even have met with him on that trip at Frank's house. But mostly I thought of him as way out of my reach. He was high up in the sky and I was a dirty worm crawling on the ground. I had started going regularly to the Methodist chapel on Sunday mornings but that was only to meet my mates and have someone to talk to. We were less likely to get nicked there than at the Church of England service.

Ten days later a screw came up to tell me I'd got a visitor. He was waiting in one of the rooms where we had our evening classes. It was Malcolm Goodman. We spent half an hour talking together. It was hard going, especially for him. A farmer and a violent thug like me didn't have anything in common. I can't remember much about our conversation – except for the last few minutes. The screw standing guard by the door looked at his watch.

'Time's up.'

My visitor put out his hand for me to shake.

'Is there anything I can get you?'

There are not that many things visitors can bring to you in prison. But there was one thing I did want. After each Sunday service in the Methodist Chapel I always came away with a copy of *The Methodist Recorder*. The chaplain handed them out to us like tracts. It wasn't a very exciting paper but when you're banged up in your peter you'll read almost anything, even a religious newspaper.

My eye was often attracted by an advert on the back page. It showed a book with a yellow cover. This, said the advert, was *The Living Bible*, written so that anyone could understand it. I'd seen plenty of Bibles in prisons. These were the ones left by the Gideons in every cell. But with their thees and thous and shalts and shalt nots they could have been written in a foreign language.

If someone as thick and uneducated as me could understand this new Bible then I wanted one.

'Have you heard of *The Living Bible*?' I asked. 'Can you
get me one?'

A smile crept across the visitor's face. He leant sideways
and reached down into a briefcase resting against his chair.
As he straightened up there were two books in his hand.
One of them had a yellow cover – it was a *Living Bible*. Of
all the books that could have been in his case, he had the
very one I'd looked at week after week in the advert. I felt
my mind start to blow. It was too way-out.

As he got up to go, he passed the two books to the screw.
'Let Brian have these when the censor's seen them.'

That was 15 August 1973. It was my birthday. I was
twenty-seven. The next evening after tea I was told I could
collect my two books.

Things had happened so fast towards the end of my
interview that I had hardly noticed the second and smaller
book he passed to the screw. All my attention had been on
that bright yellow *Living Bible*. Now, back in my cell, I
could see why he had given this other one to me.

It was a paperback. On the front cover was a knife being
held threateningly at the shirt front of some guy whose face
was out of the picture. One look at that picture was enough
to set the vibes going. The knife was about the size of the
one I used to stab the two Bognor skinheads. I opened the
pages of *Run Baby Run* and read – and kept on reading. It
was the true story of a New York gang leader. But it was
as though I was reading my story. The places were different
and the people were different but the violence and sex and
drugs and crime and hatred were the same.

The gang leader was Nicky Cruz, but he could have been
me. He left his home in Puerto Rico at fifteen. He grew up
hating his family and any kind of authority. He became a
gang leader because he was mean and bloodthirsty and
afraid of nothing. He had no heart or feeling. I knew all

the frustration and bitterness and anger that he knew. As I read, I relived my past life and could see how, like Nicky, I was on a one-way trip downwards.

I couldn't put the book down until I reached the part of the story where his life was like mine was now. We were both in a deep pit with no hope and no future and tired of running. Nicky had been told he needed love. But where, he asked, could he find real love in a pit? My God, was I in a pit. This cell was a pit. The prison was a pit. And my life was one big pit. I read on. In a crowded hall, a skinny preacher named Wilkerson was telling Nicky that God loved him. Suddenly, in front of his mates and rival gangs, this Puerto Rican double of me dropped to his knees crying.

'O God,' he calls, 'if you love me come into my life. I'm tired of running. Please change me.'

As I read how God did change him I broke down. Tears of despair and tears of hope poured down my face. The pages in front of me went blurred. Where could I find this God of love? Where could I find this Jesus who came so suddenly into Nicky's life that night, taking away the nightmares and allowing him to sleep soundly again? I needed so much to understand but I had no preacher to show me.

Then I remembered the yellow book lying beside me. If the advert kept its promise, this book would tell me all I needed to know about God, and about Jesus. I didn't know one end of it from the other. I simply opened it and read.

'I am the true vine. My father is the gardener. He lops off every branch that doesn't produce and he prunes those branches that bear fruit for even larger crops.'

It was Jesus talking about his father, God. As I read I was living the Jesus trip all over again – the same message of plants and pruning and fruitfulness. But this time I wasn't tripping. I'd had no LSD and there was no vision in white standing in front of me. Just an overwhelming feeling that God was there in my cell. I read on.

'Take care to live in me and let me live in you. A branch

cannot produce fruit when severed from the vine. Nor can you be fruitful apart from me.'

There it was. If I wanted my life to be fruitful I had to become part of Jesus. As I lay on my bed facing the door I knew that Jesus had his arms opened out towards me. He was saying, 'All you've got to do is ask me and I will change your life.' I wanted it more than anything I had ever wanted. Out loud I asked him to do for me what he had done for Nicky – to change my life, taking away all that was rotten and making it worth living.

At that instant I began to feel all the pus and poison in me drain away through my feet. All the frustration and anger that had held me a prisoner for most of my life just flowed away. At the same time it was as though a hole opened up in my head and God's love began pouring in. For the first time ever I was experiencing real love and it was God's pure love. In tears of joy I cracked up and fell to my knees on the floor, thanking God for bringing us together. After that, like Nicky, I slept a dreamless sleep – at peace with God.

I woke up with the same feeling of peace. All the bitterness and hatred had gone. I was a new person. I didn't know then that the Bible talks of being born again but that was what it felt like. I didn't understand anything about Jesus dying on a cross to save me from my sins. But I knew that somehow God was washing all the bad in me away. The stabbings and the sex and the drug-taking and, most of all, the way I had led others like Peter and Fat Mick and Smithy to become violent junkies had been forgiven. All the terrible things I had done in the past were gone. He had given me a chance to start again and I had taken it.

Never before had the world around me looked so beautiful. It was better than even the best trip and more colourful than when I had walked in the woods as a boy. In the night it had been raining. As I went out into the prison grounds to begin my first day's work as a Christian, the sun was shining and everywhere was clean and fresh. Even the black granite of the prison walls sparkled. High up the bars on the cell windows shone in the sunlight. From one part of the prison ground I could see out across the moor and down into a valley caught in the sun between shadows. In the past I had longed to be there because it meant freedom. Now it no longer mattered that I was in prison. I knew that inside myself I was free.

It didn't take long for word to get round that Greenaway had become a Jesus freak. Either I had done it to get paroled early or my mind had finally blown. All day and every day I walked around with a stupid grin on my face. I was happy but others thought that the grin just confirmed I had freaked out. I even began smiling at the screws. Perhaps, after all, they were just ordinary guys trying to do a difficult job. I felt only love towards them. It was a feeling that didn't always last. Some of the screws soon made it clear that they didn't like the change they could see in me.

Being the big mouth that I was I spent every chance I could get telling the other cons about what God had done for me that night in my prison cell. God loves you, I said. He can change your life and make it worthwhile. Some listened. Others learnt to back away when they saw me coming. One or two, like the electrician guy I worked with, had to put up with me every day. To begin with very few people I spoke to believed that the change was real but as the weeks and months went by they could see that my new faith was standing up. Much later when I'd left prison I learnt through the welfare officer that even the Governor had said everyone could see that the change in me was genuine.

From my first day as a Christian I prayed to God. It came easily. I could not sleep without it. Each evening as the lights went out and the screws moved away from the landings I knelt down beside my bed. The wing was silent. The smallest noise in another cell could be heard. I would plead with God to speak to others the way he had spoken to me. I prayed out loud but quietly for other cons by name. I prayed for the homosexual in the cell next door, not realizing that he could hear every word I was saying. And not realizing the effect my prayer was having on him.

Although I found it natural to pray I was slow in learning the power of prayer. One event really convinced me. Several months after I became a Christian I was told I had a visitor. It was a probation officer who came regularly to the Moor to see other cons. Her name was Anne Foden. I wasn't one of her clients, so why did she want to see me? She was a Christian and she had heard about my conversion. Maybe the welfare officer or one of the cons had told her.

She'd asked to see me because she wanted to hear my own version of the story. We met in the same room where the previous August I'd talked to Malcolm and he'd shown me that yellow Bible. I told her about our conversation, about the advert in *The Methodist Recorder* and about how I'd been given the two books. Then in great detail I went through my experience in the cell as I read *Run Baby Run* and how the passage in chapter fifteen of John's Gospel about the true vine brought back memories of my trip.

She listened in silence. Now and then she nodded and smiled. It was good for me to know that someone understood what had happened to me that night.

'When did all this take place?'

'About eight o'clock in the evening. It was 16 August, the day after. . .' I was going to mention my birthday but she interrupted. There was a look of excitement on her face.

'Hey, wait a minute,' she said as she took a large diary from her bag.

Quickly she thumbed through until she came to August.

'I knew it. That was the day I sat outside the prison praying,'

She explained how she had been visiting at the prison.

Then as evening came she had driven out of the gates and through Princetown. On the open road she had felt the need to pray. She pulled into a lay-by and spent nearly an hour talking to God about the prison.

'I didn't really know what to pray for or why. But I knew that God wanted me to and that I was doing the right thing. It must have been about eight o'clock when I suddenly felt that everything was all right. I stopped praying, started the car and drove home.'

Back in my cell later that day, I went on my knees and thanked God that he had used Anne and her prayers to bring me to him. And I thanked him for showing her nine months later the reason why she had been made to pray in that lay-by on the moor. It was my first lesson in how God uses people who are willing to be used. I became even more determined that I was going to be used to tell other people just how much God loves them.

13
CALL YOURSELF
A CHRISTIAN?

If I thought life was going to be easier now I'd become a Christian, I soon found out I was wrong. The first thing that happened was that I fell out with one of my best mates. He was a guy I had met in Winchester charged with being involved in a rape case. In the Moor we spent a lot of time together. At the beginning I helped him plan how he was going to rob filling stations when he got out.

When I told him I'd become a Christian and explained how different I felt he just blanked me and didn't speak to me again. Years later we met by chance in a café in London. Then he was able to see that the change in me had been real and lasting. But for the next two years until my release we remained strangers.

None of the other prisoners caused me any trouble. At least, I didn't have anyone looking out for me. It was from the screws that the opposition came. Several of them gave me stick I'd never had in prison before. They could see I had changed, and they didn't like it. A violent, paranoid Hell's Angel they could handle, but not this new guy who went around all day with a Jesus grin on his face.

Among the screws who patrolled my landing or guarded my working-party were those who watched every move I made and listened to everything I said. Often they caught me out. The change in me was not complete. Although my conversion had taken place instantly, many of my bad old habits stayed around for a long while. I had lived a rotten life full of hate and viciousness for too long. Bad language and a quick temper stayed with me. God had given me a new life but bits of the old one often showed through. They still do.

So it wasn't always easy to keep my cool when the screws started putting the pressure on me. Mostly it was only little digs about things I did or said but over the months it got heavy. And sometimes I spat back an obscene answer without thinking. The screws made the most of it.

'Call yourself a Christian, Greenaway? You're nothing but a freak.'

I'd have no trouble answering them now but then I knew nothing about the problems of being a new Christian. I had a lot to learn about the way other people treated Christians. Why should the screws of all people be upset because I wanted to live a better life? Could it be that they didn't like the idea I might go straight when I got out?

The censor screws gave me a hard time. Three or four of them read every letter that went in or out of the prison. Most prisoners' letters gave them no problems. No matter how badly written or full of porn they were, they could understand them. And if the things they said about prison life were too near the truth, they had the letter rewritten.

But they didn't know how to handle the ones I wrote. Before I became a Christian I had started writing to a place called the Coke Hole Trust. This was a drug rehabilitation centre. I knew other cons who had been there and they'd given it a good starting-price, better than Alpha House. When I first wrote, my letters were pleas for help. It was all part of my desperate efforts to get my life sorted out if I ever got out of the Moor.

Now I was a Christian I didn't need their help. God had given me the cure. I just kept writing to tell them how my life had been changed. My letters became mini-sermons. The people running the centre were Christians so, like Anne Foden, they took an interest and understood what had happened. The screws didn't. They didn't know what to leave in and what to cross out. If I got carried away and put too many of my grievances down on paper, then the censor screws really had a go at me.

Sometimes it was more than verbal aggro I had to put up with. And sometimes I didn't put up with it very well. I came near to killing one screw who pushed me too far. He was a Scot, a bit older than me and about five foot two high. A right little Hitler. When he put on his uniform he thought he was putting on muscle. He didn't like the life I was trying to live. So he killed my budgie.

Most of the cons in the Moor had pet birds. At first I thought it was soft. But it could be lonely in a cell and I soon saw how important a pet would be to a guy locked up in a peter all on his own. All the emotion and feelings he had went into his budgie. There was no other outlet in that place.

My bird was a couple of months old when the screw got it. I was beginning to teach it tricks. All the cons with birds competed with each other to see whose was the cleverest. Given the chance we exercised them out on the landing. The trick was to let them fly out over the well and call them back again before some screw came along and put a stop to it.

When the cell door was banged up in the evening the bird was my only companion. Its cage was on the table. Often if I sat writing, the cage door would be open, held back by a wire ring, and the bird would hop out and amuse itself attacking my moving pen.

The aggro between me and the Scots screw started when he was on my landing during slop-out. He let only half a dozen peters be opened up at a time. We had to slop out and get fresh water for drinking and washing from the recess on our landing in one go. Anyone having to make a second trip got a mouthful – especially me.

'Where you going you 'orrible rat? Get back in your cell.'

He seemed to enjoy trying to wind me up. As he got near, my fists would clench up tight behind me. It wasn't going to be easy to love this guy.

During the day, while we were all in our working-parties away from our cells, one of the landing screws came around testing the doors and windows. He would be looking to see that the bolts and the hinges on the doors hadn't been messed with and that no one had put a hacksaw through any of the bars. One tap with a truncheon soon gave the game away.

One day shortly after Christmas I came back to my cell for midday dinner. The bird-cage was on the table as usual but it was empty. The door was open, held back by the ring I'd made to secure it. The bird was gone. I panicked.

'Where's my b . . . b . . . bird?'

I began to stutter and swear as the old me came to the surface. Quickly I looked around the cell, first at my bunk where the bird sometimes landed after it had been flying freely. I dropped to my knees to look under the bunk. I turned my head to look around the floor. Underneath the window where it had fallen lay a piece of wire mesh. It had been knocked from the sliding vent at the top of the cell window. I looked up. The small glass vent was pushed open. I knew that my bird had flown and that one of the screws was to blame.

It was winter and outside the prison it was snowing. Inside, the central heating was full on. My bird had begun to moult and no way would it survive out there. Full of rage I dashed out through the still-open door of my cell on to the landing. All thoughts about God and of loving screws went quickly from my mind. I knew what had happened to my bird and I had a good idea who had done it. I was out for murder.

A little way along the landing, leaning over the rail and looking down into the well, was one of the few screws I had kept on good terms with mainly because he came from Pompey too.

As I came out of my cell he looked round.

'Who's been on bars and windows?' I called out to him. My voice was choked. I didn't wait for an answer.

'It was that Scotch b . . . wasn't it?'

He nodded. As I went by he grabbed me, pulling me off my feet. He was a big guy. I began to shake beneath his firm hand on my shoulder. He led me back to my cell. Other guys on the landing were calling after us. Leading me into the cell, he pulled the door and banged me up. I was alone to pace out my anger up and down my cell floor. At the sight of the empty cage and the feel of the cold draught from the opening in the window I freaked out again.

By the time the screw came back with my dinner a few minutes later I was raving.

'I'm going to have him. He's going over the top. I'll kill him!'

The screw pulled the door shut and sat himself on the edge of my bunk. First he looked at the empty cage and then at the window opening. He had worked out for himself what had happened and why I was so angry.

'You'd kill for the sake of a budgie? Is it worth it?'

Leaning forward he lit a fag and passed it to me. As I drew on it I began to calm down. He could get into trouble for what he was doing. His kindness made me begin to think straight again. I could get another budgie and, in any case, doing over a screw was about the most stupid thing a guy could do in prison. After that you never got any peace no matter what prison you went to.

Left alone in my cell I began to get angry with myself. How could I expect to convince others that God loved them and cared for them and wanted to change them if I freaked out every time someone crossed me.

It was in times like these I got a lot of strength from my

Bible reading. Especially when I read about the disciples of Jesus. It was good to find that these men were no plaster saints. They were just ordinary working guys who sometimes let him down and lost their tempers. But God still used them. He used them to start his church. He used them to change other people's lives by telling them about Jesus dying for them on the cross. Even in prison, ordinary men like Peter served God. And I wanted to do just that.

I read my *Living Bible* a lot, sometimes for three or four hours in the evening before the lights went out at nine-thirty. When I couldn't see to read any more, I prayed. Sometimes Terry Scarborough, the welfare officer, came to my cell during the midday dinner-break. We would pray together. He taught me something about prayer. I saw answers to prayer as other prisoners found the peace which I had got through becoming a Christian.

There were other Christians in the prison who helped me during the early difficult days. The Methodist chaplain who had been giving me the newspaper which started it all continued to take a great interest. He encouraged me to study my Bible. We would laugh together as he reminded me how he used to make me read the lessons during the Sunday services. Now there weren't enough hours in the day for reading it.

I didn't expect and didn't get any help from the C of E chaplain. He was more interested in keeping on the right side of the screws and cadging their drinks. I cheered as loudly as anyone the next Christmas when he announced at the concert that he was leaving. The man who took his place had no shoes to fill and nothing to lose. He couldn't help doing a better job.

When he first arrived we were suspicious of each other. I doubted him because I didn't see why he should be any better than the guy before him. And he wouldn't have known whether I really was a Christian or just conning him. He'd probably been taken in lots of times by prisoners who knew how to take advantage of an easy-going chaplain. But he didn't leave any of us in doubt about himself for very long. Within a few weeks of arriving he had visited every prisoner and knew most of their first names.

Soon he was taking an interest in our personal problems. He started an informal weeknight service he called chaplain's hour. At first only about thirty guys came along but the rowdy hymn singing which echoed through the prison block attracted more until in a short time the hall was packed with over a hundred prisoners. It was odd to see hardened criminals singing hymns at the tops of their voices. After each session we all went back to our cells feeling just a bit more like human beings. Through these meetings and in many personal ways this chaplain was able to show men that God cared for them.

14
GETTING THROUGH

I'd only been a Christian a couple of months when I got a letter telling me that six of my mates at Leigh Park had died from drug overdose. I cried my heart out, not just because guys I had known very well and had helped to become junkies were dead. But because they had died without knowing Christ as their Saviour.

One of them was a guy named Romeo. He was from the Living Dead. Even though we had been on the wrong end of each other's shot-gun more than once we got on well together. At times he was almost like a brother. As I read the letter I remembered him talking to me about God when we were tripping together. Only now did it seem important. And now he was dead.

The night I got that letter I cried for a long time in my cell. I sat staring up at the bars on the window, praying to God to let me out. I wanted desperately to tell my other mates in Leigh Park about Jesus before any more died. But there was still plenty of work to do here in the Moor and no one else but me could do it. There were guys I knew from Leigh Park in the Moor with me. First I had to tell them.

Although not Hell's Angels, several of them had known me when I was president. They knew what sort of villain I had been and could see the change. News of the deaths made me even more determined to tell as many of them as

I could about Jesus. It also made me more determined to get to know my Bible better.

Terry Scarborough and the Methodist Chaplain both helped to get me doing Bible study correspondence courses. It wasn't easy at first. My time at school had been mostly wasted. I was a back-of-the-class pupil so I had a lot of catching up to do, even with the most basic things like spelling. How was I expected to know what words like homiletics meant? It took me weeks to find out what doctrine was.

Guys in my working-party suffered the most from my early desire to tell everyone in sight about what God had done for me. There was one hippy I spoke to every day about Jesus being the best trip. Inside I got so mad because he wouldn't listen.

I kept on at him for nearly eight months. Then one spring morning as we began work, wiring two cells next to each other he came in and spoke to me.

'Hey, Brian. How many gods are there anyway?'

I found out afterwards he'd been reading the Gideon Bible in his cell. He couldn't suss out why it was God spoke of himself as 'we' and 'us'. At the time I thought he was just trying to wind me up. I didn't know the answer anyway.

'Why don't you shut up and get on with your work?'

I'm never at my best first thing in the morning, even now, so he got the sharp edge of my tongue.

A hurt look came across his face. He turned and walked out of the cell.

I'd let the guy down. With a few sharp words I had betrayed God. I remembered what I had read about Peter the disciple. Now I knew how he must have felt when he let Jesus down, pretending he didn't know him. This time I'd really muffed it. That evening I prayed hard for God to forgive me and for my workmate not to be put off by what I had said. That evening God came to his cell the same way he had come to mine. He funnelled his love into him too. Despite my temper and weakness God had used me to bring another person to Christ.

In the two years I remained at the Moor after my conversion, half a dozen guys became Christians as a result of me pestering them.

But it wasn't only in the Moor that God gave me the chance to speak to other cons. Before becoming a Christian, one of the places I'd been trying to get into was Grendon Underwood. This was a psychiatric prison hospital. One of its specialities was doing skin surgery on prisoners who had psychological problems because of their looks. Sometimes tattoos came into that class and if you had them it was considered a good skive to get them removed at Grendon.

Over the years as a Hell's Angel I had gradually covered my body with a mass of them. There were elaborate designs of birds and flowers and wild animals on my arms and body and legs. These had been done by a professional tattoo artist down by the Pompey shipyards. Others were more crudely pricked in by me during the long, tedious hours spent in other prisons. There were swastikas and snakes that looked more like worms, as well as birds of the two-legged kind.

Besides looking for a skive I had reckoned that if I could get to Grendon to have some of the more visible tattoos removed I might be kept there for psychiatric treatment because of my past drug problems. Other cons had wangled it.

Now I was told I could go and even as a Christian I wasn't going to miss a chance to get away from the Moor for a while. It was a bad time at the Moor. The screws were going on strike and there was lots of aggro. We had to spend hours at a time in the day banged up in our cells. I really did want to get rid of the tattoos on my hands. For a Christian they were out of order.

On the back of the fingers on my left hand I had pricked

out the letters H-A-T-E. Sometimes I had been asked why the letters L-O-V-E weren't on the other hand and I used to say it was because I didn't have any in me. But now things were different. I had the love of God in me. These four letters together with a ring of swastikas around each of my wrists had to come off.

For the three weeks I stayed at Grendon life was pretty easy. The only thing that really had me worried was being unconscious during the operation. I'd been unconscious before but never out of choice.

When I arrived I was put into a small ward with about six, perhaps eight, beds. There was freedom to move about the ward as well as the corridor outside and the rest of the rooms leading off. It may not have been like an ordinary hospital but it was paradise after the Moor.

There were five cons in the ward with me, all having surgery to improve their looks. One guy was having treatment for facial scars caused by burns from an exploding motor-bike tank. A couple of the others were having tattoos removed like me. There was also a guy with grotesque loppy lugs. His ears stuck straight out from the side of his head. They made him look ugly and sub-normal. It was easy to see the cause of his psychological problems. After the surgeon had taken away some gristle and moved his ears back he became quite a good-looking guy.

I was only at Grendon for a couple of hours when I had my first chance to share my faith. I'd stacked away in my locker the few things I'd brought with me and was sitting on the edge of my bed, reading. If ever I had time on my hands and no one to talk to I would read. Usually it was either the notes for my correspondence course or my yellow Bible. I hadn't noticed that someone was standing at the end of my bed.

'What are you reading?'

His straight question took me by surprise. As I looked

up, annoyed by the intrusion, I closed the book and tried to hide it.

He was a good-looking guy. Afterwards I found he was a professional actor. As I recovered from his abrupt intrusion into my reading I could see he really wanted to know what the book was.

'It's my *Living Bible*.'

I held it up for him to see. He took it in his hands.

'What you reading this for?'

'Because I'm a Christian.'

My words had an odd effect on him. With the book still in his hands he sat down on my bedside chair and started to cry. The tears rolled down his face.

'What's up?' I asked.

He poured out his problem. Soon after he got back to his prison he was due to be paroled, but that morning he had had a letter, he didn't say who from, telling him that his wife had left him for another bloke. His chief worry was that if the Governor found out he might not get his parole. He had no other home to go to.

All I could do was tell him about my new faith. Suddenly I realized that all the words were coming out right. I remembered a line of a hymn or a bit of Bible verse. I wasn't trying to be clever. I really wanted to help the guy. It was like God was giving me the words. The guy was listening and what I said seemed to help him calm down.

After that I read my Bible quite openly. Other guys in my ward began coming to me with their problems or asking me questions about my faith in God. There was something about being together in one ward day and night that made it easy to talk frankly. During that time I felt on a cloud and closer to God than at any time since my conversion. Even the doctors and the surgeon became interested as I explained why I wanted my tattoos removed. I wanted to live the sort of life where hate had no place.

Not everyone showed an interest. After my operation I

was moved to a different ward. It was divided into half-a-dozen cell-like cubicles each with its own door-way. In this ward there was less chance to talk to the other guys but at least it made it more easy for me to work on my correspondence course.

I've said life was relaxed at Grendon. But it was still a prison. Although allowances were made for guys recovering from operations, underneath the screws and cons were just the same as at any other prison. One of the guys in my new ward was a seventeen-year-old rapist. A tall and thin, evil-looking youngster with an unhealthy pimple-covered face. When he was fourteen he'd raped a very young girl, mutilated her body and killed her. He would probably be spending most of his life in prison.

Normally he would have been kept away from other cons but here at Grendon, where he was having face surgery, there was no separate place for sex cases. It was natural with a nonce around for any group of straight cons to get together to kick his head in. I'd done it before in Winchester and Chelmsford without any problem.

One day three of the other guys in the ward arrived at my door. They were going to do the kid over. Did I want to join in? When I told them no, they didn't understand it. No one took sides with a nonce in prison. But I'd been violent and sub-human too and although I despised what he had done I couldn't help feeling pity for him. The rest of his life spent in prison was going to be hell. His crime separated him from other prisoners. The only people he would be safe with were other sex cases. The screws would treat him like an animal and I knew his vile appearance would make the most godly chaplain back away from him. I had to talk to him.

'Let me talk to him first,' I said.

I was still a leader, able to get my own way with other guys. They agreed to hold off until I'd seen him.

That evening, he walked past my cell. I called out to him

by name. He stopped at the entrance, looking uncertainly into the room.

'Come in. It's OK. I want to talk to you.'

Hesitantly he stepped inside, only half-reassured by my promise that no one was going to kick his head in. He'd probably spent the last three years keeping away from cons who were looking for him. As he sat on the edge of my bed I started to talk to him about his life. I told him about Jesus and about how he'd begun to take the rottenness out of my life.

I went on at him for more than an hour, explaining how Christ had died for his sins. I showed him passages from my Bible to prove it. Most of the time there was a glazed look in his eyes. I was not getting through.

'Look, pal,' I said in desperation, 'there's no way you are going to get out of prison unless you get your head together. When you're an old man and still inside, remember that Christ has done something in my life. I was as bad and as full of evil as you. What he did for me he can do for you.'

My efforts were wasted. I prayed each night for God to speak to him. Maybe I planted a seed that has come to something since. But I don't know.

Once the scars on my hands had healed, I had no reason to be kept at Grendon. Whatever psychiatric needs I thought I had before becoming a Christian were now gone. So it was back to the Moor to finish my sentence. I felt better for my stay. Not only had some of the outward signs of my past life been taken away by the surgeon's knife; inside as well I felt that the hate that once had filled me had been replaced by love – even for guys whose lives made it difficult for anyone but God really to love and care about them.

15
COKE HOLE

After two years and eight months in the Moor I was released on parole. It meant agreeing to stay for five months at St Vincent's, the male hostel for drug addicts run by the Coke Hole Trust in Andover. The idea to go there came in the first place from the Trust's director, Barbara Henry. She had read my letters and one time visited me in the Moor.

Before my conversion I would have jumped at the chance to go there. Then I had been desperate for help. Now I wasn't so sure. I wasn't a junkie any more. I didn't think I needed any rehabilitation. God had given me the cure. All I wanted was to be free and to stand on my own feet. But it turned out to be the right place. I was soon to find out that I wasn't ready yet to go it alone. God put St Vincent's in my way as a stepping-stone between my past and my future.

With a new suit, some money and a railway ticket from Exeter station, I left Princetown by taxi in March 1975. As part of the parole-deal I had to report to a probation officer every week while I was at St Vincent's. So from Andover station I went straight to his office in the centre of the town; and straight into my first problem. After so long in prison I had difficulty relating to him. Sitting on opposite sides of his desk we spent most of the first few minutes psyching each other up. It was like a mental war between us.

He appeared younger than me, smart-looking and

smooth. To me, straight out of prison, he seemed a right Jack-the-lad trying to impress me he was tough. Give it a few weeks, I thought, and this guy would have me back inside. He had the power.

With very little talking we made an uneasy peace and he offered to drive me to the hostel. A couple of miles out of the town we turned off the road, in through high gates and up the drive of what had once been a public park. The drive went past a lake. A young guy with all the marks of a junkie was feeding ducks. There were others in ones and twos walking or sitting around a playing-field.

Eighteen years before I'd been driven to a home by my first probation officer to begin a new life. That time I'd been left to fend mostly for myself, and it all had gone wrong. This time I was going to make it. With God's help and the encouragement of the Christians, Pete and Pat Edwards, and others like them who ran St Vincent's, I knew I could.

I had no problem relating to these two – Pat's friendly smile and warm welcome and Pete's easy manner and casual way of dressing. Standing by him in my new suit and prison haircut, I was the one that looked like a straight citizen. Pete could have been mistaken for a hippy.

They knew a lot about me from my letters and Barb's visit. Right from the start they showed that they trusted me. Most of the guys staying at St Vincent's were drug addicts or ex-addicts. As an ex-junkie and gaolbird I out-classed the lot. Yet while the rules were that no one should leave the grounds of the hostel in their first month, I got out the day after I arrived.

After breakfast, as I was looking round the grounds, I got called to Pete's office.

'I'm going to London. Want to come?'

There was urgency in his voice. As he spoke he was putting on a jacket.

After two-and-a-half years in the nick, what was I supposed to say?

Pete had just had a phone call from a guy named Terry. He was a resident at the hostel who had gone away for the weekend but had been away six days. As we headed for London in his aged Escort, Pete told me about Terry. Now twenty-four, he had been a registered heroine addict since he was twelve.

From the way Terry sounded on the phone, Pete knew that he was zonked out of his head on drugs. He sounded desperate for help. He had rung from a call-box in Leicester Square. First we had to find the box. It took us three hours steady driving to reach the centre of London. Pete seemed in no hurry. I got mad because he went so slowly.

If we found the phone-box, I doubted that he would still be there. Either he would have wandered off into the side streets or, more likely, been busted by the police. Pete stayed cool as we drove round the square, while I got more and more bottled up. Pete soon spotted him. I could hardly believe it but he didn't seem surprised. Terry was standing right alongside the box he had called from nearly four hours earlier. At twenty-four, the guy looked nearer to forty. There were all the signs of addiction to heroine – the killer-drug. Receding hairline and teeth missing; vomit could be seen and smelt on the clothes which hung around his thin body. He held himself up with difficulty.

As we got out of the car and walked towards him, his bright, pin-hole eyes stared blankly at Pete. There was no recognition. He turned and looked towards me.

'You Brian Greenaway?'

I nodded in surprise. It blew my mind to hear him call my name.

'They told me you were coming.' There was relief on his face. He tried to smile. As quickly as we could we bundled him into the car.

Pete stopped to get some fish and chips and then we

drove back to Andover. On the way, Terry came out with bits of his weekend. It started OK but he'd got caught up with some junkie pals. His will to stay away from drugs broke down and he went back on the needle. Two nights he slept rough, the last night down in the underground. Why he hadn't been picked up, I don't know. Into the night people had walked around him and stepped over him, slumped in a passage way.

'No one cared.'

He kept repeating it all the way back.

'No one cared.'

His only hope had been Pete and the hostel. Pete must have known he would wait for us to find him.

Instead of going back to the hostel, we went to the cottage where Barbara and her dentist husband, Doug, lived. First stop was the bathroom. I sat on the edge of the bath watching, hardly believing what I saw. They took off his shoes and socks, washed his feet, took off his filthy clothes and cleaned him up. They talked, he listened and I watched. There was no telling-off, no angry words. Just love for a guy in the gutter. For the first time, I was seeing real Christian love in action. Barb and Doug just cared for him. To watch it was a beautiful thing.

Terry was redressed in clean clothes and fed. Then we drove him back to the hostel. Pete and Pat took it in turns to sit up with him that night. Again I was seeing the love of Christ in action.

During the first few weeks, the probation officer came to see me at the hostel. To begin with I fronted him out. Then after his second visit it suddenly clicked that it was me who was out of order. I could see the love and concern which Pete and Pat had for us all at the hostel but I saw only authority in the probation officer. Maybe I was a Christian but I was still rebelling against authority and failing to see the guy behind the job. The next time he came we talked it over. Our relationship changed dramatically and we became friends. Slowly I was beginning to see people like him differently.

I didn't always like what I saw. In his spare time the probation officer was helping the Samaritans in the town get an emergency hostel opened. They had bought a house and wanted it for people desperate to get permanent shelter. I was taken along to some of the organizing meetings. It interested me because they wanted a full-time warden to look after the place. I thought I could do the job. I even went to lectures on alcoholism and drug addiction.

At these meetings I began to see another side of Christian people in action. These were the middle-class do-gooders with a plum in their mouth, who came along because it looked good. The condescending way they made a point of asking me if there was anything they could do for me got up my nose. More than once I nearly told them to get on their bikes. I couldn't handle it so I didn't go again.

Back in the hostel I wasn't allowed to sit around doing nothing. Pete sometimes went out telling groups of people about the work of the Coke Hole Trust and his work at St Vincent's. One of these groups was the Christian Union at a teacher training college in Salisbury. I had only been out of prison three days when he asked me to go with him. I felt like some prize exhibit, living proof that the kind of weird guys he spoke about really existed.

I wanted to share my experience of God with others. But after being banged up for two-and-a-half years I was scared about going to a meeting. I felt bad enough on the way there. When I got there, I became petrified. In a small lounge filled with easy chairs were about twenty teachers, all girls and all clean and clever-looking. They were not the sort I had been used to mixing with. As Pete was being introduced I sat on a settee near the door, trying to look as small as possible.

Every now and then as Pete spoke I would look up and see some bird's face staring at me full of curiosity. At the end he spoke briefly about me, about my past life and my conversion in prison. He didn't say much. Just enough to get his audience interested in me. As he sat down he asked if there were any questions they wanted answered.

Twenty faces turned towards me. I began to lose my bottle. It was me they had come to see and I reckoned I was going to be in trouble. From the centre of the group one girl stood up. Her bright green eyes were full of fun and questions. My mind began to go blank. She was asking me to tell them more about myself. Pete grabbed me by the arm and pulled me from the settee into the front of the room. Hesitantly I began telling them my story. Pete looked pleased. This pretty-looking girl with the green eyes and posh voice was making me do what I didn't think I had the courage to do. I was telling others in public for the first time about how God had changed my life.

After the meeting that evening, the way home in the car took us through the Cathedral close. We passed a young girl walking in the same direction on the other side of the road. Pete pulled up and wound down his window. It was the girl with the green eyes.

'Can we give you a lift?'

She shook her head and went to walk on. We had been taken for strangers. He reminded her that we had just been answering her questions at the college.

'Oh, it's you!' she said, taking a closer look.

Our offer was accepted and she directed us out through the town to where she had her digs. Her name was Claire. She was a Christian. Her home was near Birmingham and she was in her last year at college. Before she got out of the car, Pete invited her to come and visit the hostel some time. I was glad he did but I never thought she would come.

While I was at St Vincent's I also had the chance to go back to Leigh Park. Pete Edwards was driving a guy from the hostel down to the courts in Pompey. I went with them and on the way back asked if we could call in on some of my old mates. I knew Pete the Animal and Smithy were around somewhere. Pete had finished his sentence before me and we had kept in touch. It was Pete who had written to tell me about the death of Romeo and the others.

Pete had done his time with me in the Moor so he knew I'd become a Jesus freak. Although I had written to him about it, I'd never really had the chance to talk to him properly about my conversion. We found him near the café working on a bike with a couple of guys I didn't know. Nothing had changed. He was back in his leathers and faded jeans. He grinned when he saw us. The same gap in his front teeth gave him the old, sinister look.

My sudden arrival had taken him by surprise but he seemed pleased to see me. Our talk got round to my letters and my conversion and he was keen to know what really had happened to me. I didn't want to miss the opportunity so I waded in. He listened quietly for a couple of minutes. Then as I started to go through what had happened to me in my cell the night I got the new Bible, he stopped me.

'Don't just tell *me*. Come back to our crash pad. The other guys are there. You can tell them as well.'

I wanted them all to know about Jesus and yet when it came to it I just chickened out. The thought of walking back into that crowd again after all that had happened scared me to death. I made some excuse about having to get back to Andover. It was a big mistake and soon I was kicking myself for it. It was to be another four years before I had the opportunity again.

16
CLAIRE

The first couple of months at St Vincent's were mostly spent getting adjusted to being out of the Moor. After the morning chore I'd be talking and walking or playing table tennis with the other in-mates at the hostel. They were mostly junkies who had kicked the habit and were trying to straighten themselves out. Other times I worked clearing the overgrown garden ready for planting. I was also given charge of a pregnant goat that had been presented to the hostel. All I got for my trouble were two baby he-goats.

Each Sunday I went to the Baptist Church in Andover. Sometimes I tried to get the other guys from the hostel to go along. I also went occasionally with Pete to a nearby village church where the people were taking an interest in the work of the Trust. The first time I went I had to stand up in front of a church full of people and tell them my story. Once I got started it came quite easily but I was very nervous. Afterwards, as I went to sit down, the minister stopped me.

'Stay there Brian. I've got someone I want you to meet.'

A big-built man got up from among the people and came to the front.

'Do you remember him?' asked the minister.

I said I didn't. Inside I began to panic. Who was this guy?

'He's an ex-policeman from Leigh Park.'

Can you imagine? That really blew my mind. Was this

ordinary-looking guy who grinned as he came towards me really one of those Leigh Park pigs I'd so often wanted to stamp my studded boots on? He put out his hand. Now there was no problem. It wasn't ex-copper and ex-villain but brothers in Christ.

I enjoyed giving my testimony in churches and talking to the young people there. But I felt the need to do more. I had more to offer. I just didn't know how to snowball it all off. It would be no use me trying to stand on a box in the middle of the street. I got cut up trying to work out the way.

While I was still in the Moor I'd had ideas about going to Bible college – even though I knew I was too thick to be a preacher. Now at the hostel it kept coming back to me. If I was to be used by God I needed more knowledge than a correspondence course could give me. For a start I thought I should learn to speak properly if I was going to put my past behind me. It never occurred to me that my rough background and the way I spoke might be an advantage in making contact with people.

Then I met the Baptist minister who came to St Vincent's to find out how it worked and to get to know the problems facing drug addicts. In the few weeks he was there we became good friends. And in the long chats this great guy gave me some good advice.

'Whatever you do, Brian,' he said one day as we sat in the hostel grounds, 'stay out of the pulpit. There are enough people there already.'

With my background and experience, he said, I could get alongside people who wouldn't come near a church or a preacher. I spoke the same language as the junkies and the ex-convicts. I should carry on writing to the guys I'd left behind in the Moor. I could go back again to the Hell's Angels and the people who suffered from them in Leigh Park. That didn't mean I couldn't go to college. I just had to be sure God was leading me there. I must learn to be patient.

It was nearly three months before I saw the girl with the green eyes again. By now I was being given a little more freedom. This particular day I had taken Pete and Pat's two young kids into the town. Some of the other guys had been out walking. They got back before us and were in the kitchen making coffee. The kitchen and the coffee jar were the popular meeting-places at St Vincent's.

Pete and Pat were there. So were half a dozen of the inmates. And in the middle of them, being chatted up, was this pretty stranger. Who was it?

I pretended not to be interested and went on making myself and the two kids some drinks. In my mind I was trying to suss out who she was. I was definitely interested but I didn't dare show it.

Realizing I was back, Pete turned towards me.

'Remember Claire?'

Suddenly, I did. It was the girl who had asked all the questions at the college. Our visit had made her interested in the work of the Trust. She had written to Barbara Henry to ask if she could come along. And now she was here. So she wasn't someone else's bird, as I thought when I first saw her in the kitchen. My interest grew. Jumping in with both feet I asked her if she would like a conducted tour of the place. We spent the rest of the afternoon looking round the house and walking in the grounds.

In the evening I took her to the station. For me, everything was clicking into place. I knew I wanted her to be my girl. At the station I pleaded to see her again. She wasn't quite so sure but before the train left she had agreed. Shortly after that Pete took me to spend the day with Claire in Salisbury. We started dating from that day.

Although by now I was allowed out from St Vincent's and was working full-time in a local diecasting foundry I didn't get the freedom I wanted. I was coming near to the end of my time here and getting restless. I wanted especially to spend more time with Claire. I'd squared it with her about my past and we'd talked a great deal about the future. We both wanted to do what was right by God. And for me that definitely meant being married to Claire. She took a bit more convincing.

Life was getting heavy at St Vincent's. The hot work I was doing pouring molten metal all day at the foundry made me irritable. I wanted to spend my spare time with Claire. The twenty-mile journey between Andover and Salisbury by train, together with the close check that Pete and Pat were still keeping on me, made me impatient to be free.

I put the pressure on Claire to find me some digs in Salisbury. As soon as my five months came to an end at St Vincent's I moved into a bedsitter near the station. Now I was doing the train journey each day between Salisbury and Andover in the other direction. At the end of the summer term at college Claire took off to visit friends. I was on my own till she got back. I even began to miss the friends at St Vincent's who had supported me during a critical time in my life.

When Claire came back I took a couple of weeks holiday and we set off hitch-hiking. I wanted her to meet some of my friends. Mostly these were the Christians in the West Country – like Malcolm Goodman – who'd helped me so much in prison. But we also went back to Leigh Park. There we stayed with my old landlady, Jacky, who was living in the same flat as before.

We knocked at the door of her flat. She was her same warm, good-natured self. I introduced her to Claire and we talked of our plans to get married. Claire went through to the kitchen and put on the kettle while Jacky and I talked in the living-room. We were just five minutes away from a miracle.

'Jacky, do you remember that time I thought I saw Jesus on one of my trips?'

She remembered and nodded.

'Well, it was.'

A puzzled expression came across her face. I started to explain all that had happened to me since the day I was arrested. I told her about Jesus coming to my cell in the Moor. And of reading in my Bible about him being the living vine. Just like my trip. I told her what it meant to be a Christian and the peace that it had brought me. The tears ran down her cheeks. What I had found she wanted as well. I called Claire back in. There on her living-room settee Jacky asked Jesus to take over her life. Before the kettle had boiled Jacky had become a Christian.

Over the next two days we learnt more about each other's lives over the last three years. Jacky had been through so much. She'd had a job driving a van for the local evening paper. Then, in a crash which put her through the windscreen, she nearly lost her arm and with it her life. But God had kept hold of her until now. And now she was a Christian. Before we left we made sure she was linked up with the local Anglican church.

Back at Salisbury we began making plans for getting married. I'd begun going to Claire's church in Downton. The minister had been at college with Claire. Our first problem was finding a place to live. And it was a problem. We searched and searched for a place to rent. The date we'd fixed to get married was in October and the time was getting very near. I'd left my job in Andover to cut down the travelling and the expense. Now I was doing shift work in a polystyrene factory outside Downton. We were getting desperate.

'How about living in a caravan?' asked Claire one evening as we searched yet another copy of the local newspaper.

No way was I going to live in a caravan. I'd spent too much of my life shut up in boxes. I didn't want it again now I was free. For several days she kept on about this caravan that was sited nearby on the edge of the New

Forest. A week before the wedding I gave in. By now I'd got a bike. I picked her up in the evening and we went off to find it. It wasn't like I had imagined at all. With the countryside all around, spacious rooms and deep windows, it was a palace compared to my bedsitter near the station and not at all like a prison.

We got married and moved in. Things went OK until I came home after a night at the factory to find Claire in tears. Alone at night in a caravan in the middle of a field, she was becoming afraid of every noise she heard. I changed jobs again. This time I was operating a drilling machine in a precision engineering firm just down the road. At last we could settle down to a steady family life. Just Claire and me. The following year we were to be joined by little Emily, two rabbits and a budgie.

As I settled down, I continued to grow spiritually. I was sharing my faith with the people at work and in particular the boss whose wife was already a Christian. Again and again during my Bible study and prayer time the idea of going to college kept coming back to me. It was like a heavy load on my back. I talked it over with the minister and with the youth leader of the church. Both said they would back me if I felt God wanted me to go.

After a false lead which took me as far as the door of a Bible college in Birmingham, I got an interview at Moorlands Bible College near Christchurch. The first time it was informal. I saw just one guy, the secretary. He was tall and stern and looked full of authority. I began to back away. If it was like this here I didn't want to come. The anti-authority in me was showing again. A month or so later I did go back, to a full-scale interview. This time it was not so informal. In a large interview-room behind a polished oak desk sat four men, the principal, two senior tutors and the secretary I'd met on my first visit.

It was a magistrates' court all over again. But this time God was in it all. I just knew this was where he wanted me to be. These men knew my background and they could probably see I was nervous. They were kindly in their questions.

'Do you have any problems with your health, Brian?' asked the principal.

'I get migraine a lot, sir,' I answered.

'That's a sign of intelligence. I used to get it but I don't any more.' We all laughed.

I began to relax, feeling that everything was OK.

Back home I told Claire and the minister I thought it was right for me to go. I didn't know where I would get the fee but when the invitation came I accepted and the following September I went back to the classroom. This time I didn't sit at the back. Now I wanted to learn. The first year was hard going. To begin with, it was getting the money. Claire and I just had to have faith that God would send it. Through other Christians, he did.

There were also some misunderstandings at my church. Because I hadn't asked for their support, many of the members turned against me. Not until I finally made it through the first year were they willing to believe that God wanted me at the college.

And hardest of all was the work. Sitting behind a desk wasn't easy after the wild life I had led. Trying to use my brain came even harder. Several times I went to the principal or my own tutor to tell them I couldn't take any more. I stamped my feet, throwing tantrums like a child. Thank God they didn't let me give up.

One of the things that kept me going was the friendship of the other students. A small group of us met together each day to talk over our work, share problems and pray. I'd always thought of the church as being like a family of bikers, each member willing to help the others. In place of the motor-cycle manual was the Bible. It was the cross instead of the motor bike and Jesus was our president.

17
WHY DON'T YOU GO?

Thoughts of those guys who had died from overdose while I was in the Moor still played on my mind. I had been partly responsible for their deaths. God had forgiven me for leading them and others astray – I was sure of that. But there would be no rest until the ones still alive – Smithy, Dog, Ali, Pete and the others – had been told about what God had done for them through Jesus.

I'd been back to Leigh Park several times since leaving St Vincent's and had met up with Smithy, Pete and Ali again. But not until I got to college did I see the rest of my old gang. It happened at a pop festival near Stonehenge – one of those fringe events that draw together the weirdest mixture of people. Junkies in a dream world and topless birds trucking around amongst Krishna converts, bikers and bead-swinging hippies.

Live music from a canvas-topped stage was only part of the attraction. Mostly it was the friendship and freedom to do their own thing that pulled in several hundred people to spend a week of days and nights together on Salisbury Plain. That meant anything from free love and smoking pot to just sitting around for hours on end meditating beneath a blue-grey cloud of marijuana smoke that hung over the field.

I went to Stonehenge at the suggestion of a biker mate from Downton. He wanted to go for the fun. I'd been to this sort of event in my previous existence and wondered what he would make of it all. For me it was the chance to talk about Jesus to people I could identify with. As we bumped our bikes over the grass track leading between rows of tents and tepees, a yellow banner caught my eye. *Jesus is Lord*, it said. At least I wasn't alone. Others were wanting to tell people about their faith. Camping underneath the banner was a group of Christians from Selly Oak.

During the festival I came back several times. It was only twenty miles from Downton, so I went home to Claire each night. In the day I met up with the students and we would go out in pairs, talking to anybody willing to listen and giving leaflets to those who weren't. Part of the time I spent taking photos – to show the people back at college and church that there was this other world out here.

It was while I was out taking sneak shots with my telephoto lens that I first saw my old mates together in one place again. About twenty of them were camping at the edge of the field with their wives and birds. A pain came into the pit of my stomach as I saw their tents and shining bikes, cars and vans. Among them were several hangers-on, mostly bikers or guys I had known from the Living Dead. Bert was there, and nearby his Alsatian, Tristan. The chapter had changed since he had taken over from me as president. In my time we would not have mixed with straight bikers. I drew the line at the Living Dead.

Bert had changed too. He was married now and had a couple of kids. His whole family was there, camping in the back of a van. He still wore his leathers and studded belt but he was much less aggressive than in the old days. At first he didn't seem pleased to see me. All the while we talked he was psyching me up. I was an intruder on his patch. Maybe he thought I wanted my old job back. But we got on OK, talking about old times. Getting around to the new times wasn't so easy.

The student I'd been touring the camp with, stood a little way off, watching us with deep interest.

'Hey,' I shouted across to him, holding out my camera. 'Come and take a picture of me and my mate.'

Bert backed off and looked puzzled. Hell's Angels didn't like having their pictures taken, not even by ex-Hell's Angels.

'What do you want that for?' he asked suspiciously.

'To show me doing my work.'

'What work's that?'

'Giving out these things,' I replied, taking a leaflet out of my shoulder bag and handing it to him.

At last I'd broken the ice. I began to explain. He'd heard from Smithy that I'd gone religious but now he got the lot. I spent the next hour telling him about my Saviour. I sensed that he was taking it all in but we parted without making any real progress. All I had for my trouble were a few more pictures to add to the collection. I did not know it then but that meeting was the beginning of a kind of friendship at a deeper level than we had known before.

At the pop festival I also met Gary again. This was the guy with the musical rocking-chair whose front room we'd been in on that Jesus trip. Since the last time we met, before my conversion, he had been to India and started experimenting with drugs no one back home knew much about. He'd become a superweird guy, part junkie and part tramp. Speaking to him I found it hard to hold his attention. I would catch his eye for just a few seconds at a time. Then he'd look down at the grass at his feet, or become absorbed in the strangely-carved walking-stick in his hand. Most of the time he was off in a world of his own, his mind fully blown.

I had already heard from Bert that Smithy had come under Gary's influence as some kind of disciple. To watch Gary now, suspended between two worlds, made my heart ache for Smithy. He was a special guy to me. It hurt to think he might finish up like this. I'd lost touch with him since I'd been in college but we met here again at the festival. He was trucking around the field high on pot and having problems trying to get it together. Seeing him making a wreck of his life made me even more determined to get the gospel to the people of Leigh Park.

I learned a lot in the time spent at Stonehenge, as well as at similar events later in Glastonbury and Bolton. People were willing to listen if you had something worth saying. But you had to be dead straight with them. Many I spoke to knew at least as much about Christianity as a religion as I did. They soon saw through any weak arguments. It was only by talking of my own experiences of Jesus as a living and personal friend that I made any impression. That was the experience I wanted to share with all these beautiful people at the festival, as well as those who lived in Leigh Park.

Back at college I got the names of evangelists and preachers who might be talked into taking a mission on the estate. One after another their answers came back – they didn't want to know. They'd either seen how big Leigh Park was or they had heard of its reputation as the evangelist's graveyard.

Then towards the end of my second year at college, a guy came to lecture us on evangelism. Straight away I went to see him. I told him about Leigh Park and about how heavy I felt for all the people there. I described how it had been when I lived there as a Hell's Angel. Of how decent people lived, unreached by the few local churches but continually aggravated by gangs like mine. And there were youngsters still growing up under the influence of petty thieves, thugs and drug addicts.

Would he think about taking the gospel to these people by holding a mission there? He listened patiently. At last I was getting through to somebody. But I didn't get the answer I was hoping for. His reply shook me rigid.

'Why don't you go?'

It seemed so obvious, and so right. Why hadn't I thought

of it before. In fact there were quite a few reasons why I hadn't allowed the idea any room. What did I know about running a mission? Admittedly I'd spoken at church rallies, but that wasn't the same as confronting my old mates and their apathetic families and neighbours in any big way. Mostly it was because I was scared for my life. I still had lots of enemies in Leigh Park and places around it. Some of them were very handy with knives and shot-guns. I could probably handle one at a time but if they came down team-handed I'd soon get carved up – and they had plenty of reason for doing it. There were some parents who had no cause to love me either.

I went back to my room and prayed it over. The more I prayed the more right it seemed. I didn't have any confidence in myself. That would have to come from God. And it would be up to him to give me the protection too. I knew I had to go. After all, I owed it to the people of Leigh Park for all the aggro I'd caused them in the past. And hadn't I been told that I was the one who spoke the right language to reach them with God's good news?

I talked it over with the lecturer in greater detail. I would need some help and I would have to learn to delegate while still staying in charge. It was like being president again – this time of heaven's angels and with God in charge instead of the Devil.

First I shared my concern for Leigh Park with the other college students. One lunch-time in the dining-hall after our meal I took courage and stood up in front of the eighty or so students. I told them what I believed God was calling me to do and ended up by asking for ten volunteers. I wanted people to knock on doors, hand out leaflets around the local shops, run a coffee bar and share in a week or so of nightly meetings. Very quickly I got all the help I needed. God was at work.

The next problem was finding somewhere to hold the meetings. I didn't know where to begin. Then I remembered Betty Bell. She had been mentioned when Claire and I had been to see Jacky. It was a name I knew well – a name out of my past. I'd known she was a churchy type when I lived at Leigh Park. Would she be willing to help me now? In those days we had been on opposite sides of the fence in more ways than one.

Mrs Betty Bell was a magistrate and during part of my stay in Leigh Park had been my next-door neighbour. In those days she was high on the list of people I had a hate for. And not just because she sat on the magistrates' bench. I was sure that whenever I got nicked for having no tax or insurance on my bike it was Betty Bell who grassed on me to the law.

Her kids used to get on my nerves too. Working nights, I got woken up regularly during the day as they played and shouted in the garden next door. I often freaked out and retaliated. One time I put my bike on full throttle in the back garden and left it running for twenty minutes – until a copper appeared over the fence and sent me diving for cover indoors.

How different things were now. It had got round that Greenaway had been converted in prison, so although my visit to her was a surprise she gave me a warm welcome as she opened the door. I went in with some apprehension but we had a lovely time. She listened excitedly as I told her my story. Then I outlined what I believed to be God's plan for Leigh Park, together with some of the problems that went with it – like finding somewhere to hold the mission.

Immediately she suggested the Baptist Church next to 'The Rover' public house. I knew the pub well. I knew all the pubs in Leigh Park. But there was no Baptist Church next to this one. She assured me there was and that it had been there a good few years. I argued black and blue against her but of course she was right. I'd just never seen it.

So I went to see the minister of the church. I explained it all over again. He promised to share it with his deacons and church members and let me know. Although he might have heard of me and my past, he had come to Leigh Park after I'd left for my long holiday, so he had no firsthand knowledge. But I knew there must be some members there who did. He must have convinced them that my request was genuine because they agreed to our team having free use of the church and its halls and kitchen for ten days leading up to Easter. It meant that we could eat and sleep on the premises. We could use them as a base for going out into the estate around as well as for a coffee bar, with evening rallies held in the church itself.

That was in the autumn of 1977. During the next few months I paid a lot of visits to Leigh Park, meeting the local Christians and making plans for printing and publicity – as well as making a bit of publicity of my own. Although it was Jesus and not me we were going to preach about, I made the most of my Hell's Angel background to get people interested in the mission. Leaflets showed ex-Hell's Angel Brian Greenaway surrounded by a crown of thorns. The crown of thorns was right, first because it showed the suffering of Christ at Easter and second because a very large model of the crown hung from the ceiling of the Baptist Church.

During my visits to Leigh Park I kept my promise to see Smithy again. A couple of weeks before the mission was due to start, Smithy and I spent the day together on nearby Hayling Island. On the way over we stopped off to have a ploughman's lunch. Surrounded by the noise and bustle of a crowded pub, I had my first chance to get down to some serious talking. As we sat on opposite sides of a tiny table, I could see in his eyes the loneliness that I had often known during the last months as president of the Leigh Park Hell's Angels.

He too was crying out for help. We talked of the trips we'd been on and, in particular, my Jesus trip. His had been a bad one that day but he remembered mine well enough. From there we went on to talk about my life in prison and how that life had been completely changed since the evening I'd felt God's love come funnelling in. As I spoke his eyes filled with tears. In that crowded place God was speaking to him. He'd reached rock-bottom – the place where God is most able to help. There and then a transformation began to take place as he asked Jesus to control his life, remove his dependence on drugs and make him a new creature. It was an experience soon to be shattered for him by over-enthusiastic Christians, but at the time I saw it as another encouraging sign for the mission ahead.

18
FULL CIRCLE

Every night of the ten-day mission was special. And nearly every night was lovely. Although we had some idea of what we would be doing each day, it was all very basic. But then so was the message we had come to share with the people of Leigh Park. *God loves you enough to send his Son to die for you. All he wants is for you to accept the forgiveness he offers through Jesus.* That was it.

Even though we were pretty green and lacked experience, God used us. Out in the streets, in the evening mission meetings and in the coffee bar afterwards, we were able to reach the ordinary people with that message. Eighteen people gave their lives to God. And many others were challenged. On most evenings, after the singing and the testimonies and after a gospel group had played, I spoke for a quarter of an hour or so, telling the usually full church what it meant to have a new life through believing in Jesus.

At the end, while everyone's head was bowed in prayer, people were asked to put up their hands if they thought God had been speaking to them. I never made any long appeals. I don't believe in begging people to become Christians. Being a Christian isn't that easy. And if it's forced the experience doesn't usually last. When people came forward after the meeting to speak to the team, I left the job to others. I knew that some people had come out of curiosity just to see ex-Hell's Angel Brian Greenaway. We'd aimed the publicity that way but I didn't want any of them saying afterwards, 'It was Greenaway who converted me.'

My fears of a shoot-out during the mission came to nothing. The nearest we got to any trouble was when we showed the film *The Cross and the Switchblade*. This powerful and sometimes violent film tells the story of the New York gang leader Nicky Cruz from the angle of Dave Wilkerson, the preacher used by God to bring him to Jesus. The evening we showed the film the Leigh Park Hell's Angels and some of their hangers-on turned up in force – thanks to Bert, their president.

We had already seen Bert several times at the church during the mission. Once he called in during the day on his way to collect his dole money. Another time he brought his wife and two young daughters along to have tea with the team. We told him what the film was about and he promised to put pressure on the rest of his guys to come along. He already knew what a big influence the Nicky Cruz story had had on my life.

Sure enough, the gang came and filled the front rows of the church. They also filled some of the straight citizens with fear. The sight of these black-jacketed, long-haired and unclean layabouts with studded belts and heavy boots must have been even more frightening inside a clean and brightly-lit church than outside in the road sitting on their bikes.

I got a bit worried myself. Mostly because the film would cost a lot of money to replace if it got damaged. But deep down inside I was glad and excited to see them. These guys were the main reason for us being here. No one had told me about Jesus when I'd lived here in Leigh Park. It had taken a four-year stretch in prison to bring me face to face with him. As they came down the aisles of the church to the front I shot a quick prayer to God, first that he would speak to them through the film and second that there would be no trouble.

It wasn't the guys I knew that worried me. Most of my old mates had got used to the idea of me being a Jesus freak after we met at the pop festivals. It was the ones I didn't know that bothered me. There was one guy who came in with the others but didn't sit with them. He preferred the back of the church. At the start of the meeting he pulled out a porn magazine from inside his jacket. It kept him occupied for most of the next hour and a half. Only now and then did he lift his eyes from the pages to look at what was going on around.

I'd seen *The Cross and the Switchblade* film several times. Each time it excited and challenged me over again. My mind would go back to that cell in the Moor. I got a mental flash of Nicky Cruz's own book *Run Baby Run* with its stiletto knife on the front cover. Now, as the story was shown on the screen, I kept looking out to see how all these guys were taking it. In the light of the projector I watched for their reactions, expecting, I suppose, some sort of miracle to take place. In turn they whistled and fidgeted, stamped their feet or sat in silence without moving. Then in the interval, as reels were changed and the people around them began talking, the whole gang got up and walked out. All except Bert who was left behind staring after them, surprised and angry.

Afterwards he asked them if the film had been too heavy for them. Couldn't they take it? It wasn't that, they said. The truth was they had been bored with it. The violence had obviously meant nothing to them and the message from the preacher in the film had gone right over their heads. It turned out that several of them had already seen the film – in the nick. They had only come, they said, either because Bert had asked them or out of curiosity to see me.

When the others left, the guy reading the magazine stayed in his seat. He didn't move even after the second half of the film was finished and I was telling them how my life had changed in the same way as Nicky's. As I spoke of

God's love funelling into my life I had a powerful feeling of love towards all the people sitting in the rows of seats in front of me. And I told them so. At the same time I felt pity and sorrow for the guys who had already walked out. I kept that feeling to myself.

After the meeting I stood at the back of the church, shaking hands with the people leaving. The guy with the magazine stood up and moved towards the aisle leading to the door. As he did, he pulled a packet of cigarettes from his pocket, struck a match and lit up. I watched, sensing that it was being done to aggravate me. This guy was putting my claims about loving to the test. He moved towards me, dropping the used match on the floor of the aisle. I began to freak. This was God's house. No way could I tolerate it.

'Excuse me, friend.' I spoke slowly, trying not to show I was bottled up. 'There's no smoking in here. It's an insurance risk.'

'So what?'

There was no aggro in his voice. Just a flat, 'So what?' I reckoned that through him Satan was trying to put me to the test. I didn't know how I was going to handle it. I called across to one of the members of the church who had been helping during the mission. He was a strong and experienced Christian, who played the piano for us and helped with the publicity. Perhaps he could explain the rules to this guy.

He started to walk over. I turned my head again to face the guy with the cigarette. As I did he took it from his mouth and spat on the floor. My boasting of love was really being put to the test. I felt myself freaking out. The temptation was to kick him in the mouth. But I forced myself to cool it.

For the next fifteen minutes we tried to reason with the guy, at the same time edging him closer to the door and into the forecourt outside. Each of those minutes was a trial. Every move he made and everything he said seemed intended to provoke me. If I gave in now to the aggro inside me I would have to hit him and the rest of the mission would be ruined. Instead, I fought the battle inside myself. Only after we threatened to call the police did he go away.

I felt shattered. All the strength had drained from me as though I had been working hard physically. Getting into my car I drove down to the waterfront at Portsmouth. I parked and spent the next hour in the car looking out over the water, watching bobbing lights in the distance with tears in my eyes. Anger over what I had been tempted to do was mixed with a sense of gratefulness that God had kept me from doing it. Eventually I calmed down, started the engine and drove back to Leigh Park and the church.

All except one room of the church was in darkness. The coffee bar we ran after each evening's meeting was closed and the people had gone home. In the room with the light I knew the team would be together talking over the day, and making plans and praying for the work tomorrow. These informal meetings sometimes went on into the early morning. I couldn't face it. Instead I went straight to the room where as team leader, I slept by myself.

The film evening was the only evening that brought disappointment to me, as well as near disaster to the mission. All the rest of the meetings were a great time. Each one was different. One evening we had a sketch with all the members of the team taking part. There were also testimonies from church members. And the gospel group was very popular.

Most of the eighteen people who came forward during the meetings to give their lives to Jesus were in their teens. But not all of them. The mission finished on Easter Sunday with a baptismal service taken by the minister of the church. As well as those who came regularly to the Sunday services, there were a lot of people who had been at other meetings during the mission. By then we had got to know some of them very well. We reckoned we had a good idea which ones God had been speaking to and who was being challenged.

The church held about 250 and that Sunday night it was almost full. As on every other night, before I closed in prayer I asked if there was anybody who had felt God speaking to them during the meeting.

'As we pray I want you to put up your hand if you do. The rest of you keep your eyes down. No peeping.'

In the church were two teenage girls who had been every night to the mission and to the coffee bar. The team had made friends with them and I felt sure God had been challenging them. This would be the last chance for them to come out into the open. But they didn't move. They remained with their heads bowed. Instead the hands of two older people went up. One was a woman on my left and the other a man on my right.

The woman was in her mid-twenties, the wife of a Hell's Angel who had been at one time a rival of mine. Every night she had been at the meetings, sent by her old man to check me out. He had wanted to know what sort of stunt I was trying to pull. Instead, God checked her out and she became a Christian on the last night of the mission.

The guy was a bit older. He had recently been released from Broadmoor and was finding life very hard. Each week he had to report to a probation officer and because of this hadn't been able to get a job. Like me, he was reached by God when he was at rock-bottom. As I told my life-story during that evening it all made sense to him. God picked him up and gave him a new life with meaning again, even though things for him were not going to get any easier as a Christian.

My biggest disappointment of the mission was Smithy. For me his conversion over that lunch-time ploughman's had been a sign that the mission would go ahead. I had given him a *Living Bible* and put him in touch with a lively church. Take care of him, I said, he's a special mate of mine. The trouble was, they went overboard. He wanted to know all there was to know about his new faith. The Bible says that New Christians should be fed on milk. But very soon they were trying to get him to eat meat. He got spiritual indigestion and quickly gave up in despair.

In spite of such disappointments, mostly with the Hell's Angels, I believe the mission itself was a success. God used it and the team to speak to many of the people I had wanted to reach. These people would never have come into a church at any other time. And nobody in Leigh Park could have been in any doubt why we were there or what had happened in my life since the day I had gone away on my long holiday. Many who didn't come to the mission heard me on Radio Victory or read my story in the local Portsmouth daily paper.

If the mission created any problems, they were back home in Downton with Claire and me. I hadn't wanted her involved in the mission in case there was trouble. And she had enough to do at home looking after little Emily. When it was all over I kept going back to Leigh Park regularly. Mostly it was to see the new friends I'd made and to help the converts as well as follow up others who had been challenged at the mission. These included Bert, whose two girls had shown an interest in going to Sunday school.

All of this was on top of driving fifty miles each day to college and back and speaking at meetings in the evenings. Sometimes on the way home from college I would stop off to see friends in Ringwood. We would share news or have a time of prayer together. When I eventually got home it was late and so Claire didn't get any of the news. I was neglecting her. We were not spending the time we needed in prayer and Bible study together. Over and over again the words of a Bible text would come back to me; *Rejoice in the Lord*. But it seemed so difficult to do. After the excitement of the mission I couldn't settle down to routine. Things were beginning to get uncomfortable.

Then, on a wet road coming home from college with two other Christians and a hitch-hiker we had just picked up, I smashed up my car. The lorry in front of us braked to avoid another car. We were too close and as I put on the brakes we slid straight under the tail end of the lorry. Although none of us was hurt, the car was off the road for several weeks. During that time getting to college was a nightmare of buses and trains. I was forced to spend more time at home with Claire.

God was teaching Claire and me a lesson. Before we could serve him properly in the world outside, things had to be right at home. It was as though God had drawn back from us until we were prepared to get things together again. We heard the warning and rededicated our lives together to him. I was still uncertain about the future, but God had it all worked out. He was making sure that we were ready to do what he wanted.

EPILOGUE: A NEW BEGINNING

The mission at Leigh Park really took my life full circle. What happened after that was just as exciting, but it was the beginning of a new story. There is one more thing, though, to round this chapter of the story off:

Even before going to Moorlands College I had been challenged about working for the London City Mission. The minister of our church in Downton had been a London City Missionary himself, and suggested that it would be the right place for me. My answer was – no way! I did want to work among ordinary people, but not in London. We lived just half a mile away from the beautiful New Forest. Claire and I loved it there. And it was a perfect place for Emily to grow up in, with the open space and fresh air. Not to mention the ponies.

I was at home there. Although many memories of my boyhood in a country village were painful, I was always a country boy. Just the thought of living in London sickened me. I remembered going to Oxford Street with Claire to buy my wedding suit. Dust floated in the air and grit ground between our teeth. Living day after day in that was not for me.

At the end of my first year at college a London City Missionary came to tell the students about the work. He spoke frankly about his job and the needs of the people living in London. He also told some moving stories of lives being changed through the work of individual missionaries. I felt compelled to check it out and went to speak with him afterwards – not that I had any plans of getting tied up with the LCM. I didn't want anyone on my back or leaning over my shoulder watching what I was doing. I couldn't work for an organization like that.

Then in the second term of my third year, with the Leigh Park mission already over, the college secretary told me I'd been booked to spend two weeks working with the LCM as part of my practical training. Suddenly, out came all the excuses. At that time Emily was getting over whooping cough and Claire seemed unwell. They couldn't be left on their own for two weeks. I just didn't want to go. What God might have wanted didn't seem so important.

Desperate for a way out, I went to see my personal tutor.

In his office I tried all the grovelling and pleading I knew. But he wouldn't have any of it. I was going and that was that. Seeing that there was no use arguing, I agreed to go. After all, it was only for two weeks. Let me get in and get it over with. As soon as I gave in I began to have peace.

The first week was spent at Hoxton with a missionary who had his own mission hall. That first week I discovered he didn't have anybody looking over his shoulder. He was left to get on with doing just what he thought was right. He was his own boss, answerable first to God. So, many of my old ideas about the LCM being a kind of big brother went out of the window.

The second week was very difficult. I spent my time with several street missionaries, working in Covent Garden fruit and vegetable market, Smithfields meat market and amongst the down-and-outs on the Thames Embankment. For the first time my eyes were opened to the spiritual needs of the ordinary people in London and of the deprived who had come here to escape from their past. I found out that it wasn't only convicts who lived in prisons.

During the two weeks, I stayed in the Mission's own hostel. The eight or nine other guys there at the time were all candidates doing their initial four months' training. I found out later that they were all praying I would join them as a candidate for the Mission. I didn't tell them I'd been praying 'Please, God, get me out of here!' But it was becoming more difficult to clear from my mind the idea that God wanted me here in London.

There was a continual conflict. I was willing to be interviewed by the candidate secretary. But all the time I was hoping he would turn me down. When I didn't get turned down there seemed no way of escape. Back home in Downton I talked it over with Claire. She felt I was being called by God to work with people one-to-one but she was even less keen than I was to live in London. Reluctantly, we agreed that instead of completing the last term of my third year at college I should spend a four-month trial period with the Mission as a candidate. The college had no objections and I didn't have the course fees anyway.

I began my training during the Easter of 1979, just one year after the Leigh Park mission. Leaving Claire and Emily back in Downton I arrived at the LCM headquarters near Tower Bridge on Monday 23rd April. There I was introduced to Basil Norgate, who ran a large mission of eighty members in Ealing. He was to be my trainer, right through a remarkable summer.

My four months at Ealing stretched to five. I began to get edgy. Everyone else in the mission seemed to expect that I would stay. My work amongst the people had helped me to see their needs. It had also shown me what I could do to help. But I still wanted to get out of London. As I talked each day to God I began laying down conditions. For a start I didn't want to work under another missionary, running someone else's mission hall. And I didn't want to work out in the streets away from my family. If I didn't get my own hall I wasn't going to stay. And if I did get one it would have to be a tough one with plenty of challenge.

God answered my prayer. After the candidate's board had met I was offered the job of running my own hall – on the Isle of Dogs. This two square miles of land, held in a horseshoe bend on the River Thames, is right in the heart of London's deserted East End dockland. I couldn't have asked for a tougher place. God has his sense of humour.

Claire, Emily and I moved into the flat above the mission hall in Glengall Grove early in September 1979. From the first floor living-room, filled with furniture given to us by so many friends, we looked out over our new surroundings. In one direction were the backyards of run-down council flats. In the distance motionless cranes stood on the skyline beyond a graffiti-covered footbridge. A second window looked out over the mud-chute, a vast wasteland of hard earth and stunted trees built up over the years as the river had been dredged. Through the living-room door and across the landing a window overlooked the concrete-and-asphalt playground of the school next door.

It was all so different from the open countryside we had been used to. But there was an inward peace which Claire and I silently shared as we explored our new home together. Surrounded by apathy, vandalism and the misery of people put out of work, we had a lot of battles ahead of us. Much of the time would be spent picking up those who had been mentally and spiritually wounded and knocked down. Often it would be the same people over again.

In the past I had fought in many violent, selfish and senseless battles. I had hurt and physically wounded other human beings. How different it all was now. This was God's battle we were fighting. A battle of love instead of hate. In place of the studded boots and razor-sharp knife I was learning to rely on God's weapons and his protection. At last I could feel that the bad past had been put behind me and that here in the heart of London a new way of life was about to begin.